RESUMPTION AND THE DOUBLE STANDARD;

OR,

THE IMPOSSIBILITY OF RESUMING SPECIE PAYMENTS IN THE UNITED STATES WITHOUT RESTORING THE DOUBLE STANDARD OF GOLD AND SILVER.

A SPEECH DELIVERED IN THE SENATE OF THE UNITED STATES, APRIL 24, 1876,

BY

JOHN P. JONES,

SENATOR FROM NEVADA.

"To annul the use of either of the metals as money is *to abridge the quantity of circulating medium*, and is liable to all the objections which arise from a comparison of the *benefits of a full, with the evils of a scanty, circulation.*"—Alex. Hamilton. (Report to Congress, 1791.)

WASHINGTON, D. C.
M'GILL & WITHEROW, PRINTERS AND STEREOTYPERS.
1876.

RESUMPTION AND THE DOUBLE STANDARD.

Mr. JONES said:

Mr. PRESIDENT: The act of February 12, 1873, now incorporated in title XXXVII of the Revised Statutes, an act which, under the guise of regulating the Mints of the United States, practically abolished one of the precious metals, was a grave wrong; a wrong committed no doubt unwittingly, yet no less certainly in the interest of a few plutocrats in England and in Germany, and as certainly in the interest of the entire pagan and barbarian world; a wrong upon the people of the United States and of the whole civilized globe; a wrong upon industry, upon the natural tendency of wealth toward equalization, upon the liberties of peoples which are born out of the effects of such equalization of wealth, upon every aspiration of man which depends for its realization upon the development of those liberties.

The act alluded to, practically abolished one of the precious metals as money, the one chiefly produced in this country, the one chiefly consumed in the semi-civilized countries of Asia, and the one which at the date of its abolition and under the time-honored laws that previously prevailed, was becoming, as it has since become, the more available metal of the two in which to transact exchanges and liquidate debt.

Under the act of April 2, 1792, both silver and gold coins—dollars or their multiples—were made a legal tender in this country for the payment of debts to any amount, at the rate of 15 in weight of silver to 1 of gold. This co-ordination of silver and gold is called the double standard. A similar arrangement existed in the other countries of the civilized world; the relation fixed by law in those countries being either 15½ or 16 for 1. A few countries had a single silver standard, but no country, until 1816, had a single gold standard. In this country, up to 1853, the Government defrayed the expense of manufacturing coins, whilst in Europe, except in England, where the coinage is also free, the owners of the bullion offered for coinage are assessed with a charge for manufacture. Thus, under our old laws, and, as I shall endeavor to show, under the requirements of the Constitution, the owner of either gold or silver bullion had the right, if the Government chose to coin any money at all, to have his bullion coined free of charge; and once coined it became a legal tender to any amount for the payment of debts, whether the bullion was of gold or silver.

Although free coinage only dates from that era of other free institutions, the American Revolution, the double standard of money has existed since the remotest past. This arrangement, so far as we know, has existed everywhere and forever, notwithstanding the fact that at certain periods silver as compared with gold is yielded by the mines in deficit of the world's consumption, whilst at other periods gold, as compared with silver, is yielded in deficit. At the period in question—that is to say, from 1792 until the effects of the discovery of the Russian, the American, and the Australian gold mines were felt—gold was produced in deficit; and by reason of this fact, silver, at the legal rate of 15 for 1, was the cheaper metal in which debts could be discharged. Accordingly, silver was used for this purpose in this country to the exclusion of gold, the debtor being at liberty to tender either metal he thought proper. By the act of June 28, 1834, this relation was changed to 16.00215 for 1, and by that of January 18, 1837, to 15.98837 for 1, in both cases substantially 16 for 1, at which figure it stood up to February 12, 1873.

When the great Russian mines threw their auriferous products upon the markets, gold became the cheaper metal at the legal relation of, then, substantially, 16 for 1, and our silver legal-tender dollar disappeared from circulation. Nevertheless this coin was not abolished, and the privilege of free coinage and the right to tender the silver dollar for debt remained the same as before. The pivotal point of this event was the period of depression which followed the panic of 1837. About the period 1863–'73 another great change in the relative production of the metals occurred, and gold instead of silver was produced inadequately. This occurrence began to operate about the year 1865, when the world's product of gold had attained its maximum. However, this change did not appear to have been felt until some few years afterwards, when its influence upon the relative value of the metals was greatly intensified by the threatened demonetization of silver by the German Empire and its partial actual demonetization by other European States. In 1865 the relation of gold to silver in the London market was 1 to 15.33; in 1872 it was 1 to 15.63. This is considered the pivotal point of the change, because the legal relation of gold and silver in most of the countries of Europe was 15.50. In 1874 the London quotation rose to 16.15, and at the present moment it is about 17.60, a relation which shows that the value of gold to silver is about 10 per cent. above that fixed by our law of 1792, as amended by the acts of 1834 and 1837.

The double standard, or the legal establishment of a fixed relation between silver and gold, at the calculated center of their mutual oscillations, is not the unnatural and one-sided measure which some recent writers have supposed it, but the fulcrum of a just balance whose scales are alternately depressed. Both gold and silver are indispensable, and needed for the coins of the world—gold for large payments, silver for large and small ones; and it will be found that in great commercial countries both gold and silver are needed. Outside of the great bulk of mankind who use either one or both of those metals for money, there is a small number on the one side who are too poor even to use silver, and a small number on the other who are too rich even to use gold. The very poor employ copper, the very rich paper notes and checks. In both of these cases the substitutes for gold or silver are not real money, but representatives. Copper coins are never of full weight, and are called tokens; paper instruments are intrinsically worthless, and are merely promises, direct or remote, to pay money of gold or silver. To the mass of mankind gold and silver are both indispensable for the purpose of exchange, and these two metals constitute the money of the world.

Were their quantitative relation unknown or changing always in one direction—for example, was silver always becoming cheaper or gold dearer—a double standard would prove inconvenient. But such is not the fact. The relation of these metals to one another for many centuries has been very constant, the pivotal point being 15½, and the oscillations—until within the past year, and chiefly in consequence of the demonetization of silver in Germany—quite inconsiderable. This constancy of relation is due to the stock of precious metals already in the world, to the proportion of gold to silver needed for the world's convenience, to the vicissitudes of production, to the occurrence of gold and silver in the same ore matrices, and to other physical circumstances which will be adverted to hereafter.

Without, perhaps, fully knowing the causes of it, but assured from long experience of its continuance, nations have hitherto been satisfied, in their search for an approximatively immutable measure of values, to adopt the double standard, which, constituting a measure, now of gold and then of silver, nevertheless served to measure with constant efficiency any given quantum of labor or its products; just as a peck measure, whether constructed of gold or silver, will measure always just one peck, or as nearly so as the different effects of temperature upon the two metals will permit.

This is what has been understood in all ages by the double standard, and this is what our forefathers understood by it when they fixed it, first at 15 and then at 16 to 1, a wise and far-sighted mean between the market relation of silver and gold for two generations previous to and after the date of the three enactments which they transmitted to us.

In case no such amendments had been made to the bill now before the Senate, as have been offered by the Senator from Missouri, it was my intention to offer a simple amendment to restore the double standard of the United States, and to base its system of money upon the money of the world, upon which it is now not based. To accomplish this object it was suggested that I might with perhaps greater assurance of success attempt it by the same indirection which practically destroyed the double standard. But this course might indicate a lack of confidence in the strength of the amendments or the sufficiency of those arguments of sound policy and expediency upon which they rest.

The wrong which has been done can never be fully undone by indirection. The undoing must be as open and explicit as the doing was indirect and implied.

To secure this result nothing more is needed than that the history of the precious metals shall be recalled; that history which is so full of happiness and misery, of affluence and of poverty, of ease and of hardship; that history in part of which my life has been passed, and which has, therefore, impressed itself upon me not only by study but partly also by practical experience.

The flood of light which this history throws upon the subject, while it will establish the necessity and importance of the double standard, will also serve to allay any fears that may be entertained, on the one hand, as to the observance of specie contracts, or, on the other, as to the due recognition of paper credit as an economical and essential element of the currencies of modern nations.

As this history, be it ever so briefly recounted, is of some length, and as the conclusions to which I desire to direct attention are somewhat numerous, I deem it best at the outset to summarize what I propose to say on this subject.

First. I propose to set forth the function and nature of Money, the various substances which have been used for money, and the characteristics which during fifty centuries of trials have induced the precious metals as a duality to be always resorted to for this purpose throughout the world.

Second. I propose to show that the use of money and the preference of the precious metals for money were both natural and voluntary acts, not due to law or edict, and that, therefore, money is of right, and ought to be, free and untrammeled by any regulations except of a kind specified.

Third. I propose to trace the stock of the precious metals in the world from the earliest period for which we have authentic data, to show its mutations down to the present time, and the political, industrial, and social phenomena which accompanied those mutations. From this review I expect to be able to show that the world's stock of specie, which is now of great magnitude, consists nearly one-half of silver; that any diminution or disuse of such stock, whether resulting from failure of the mines or arbitrary legislation, is fraught with the greatest disasters which can befall society; and that, therefore, the two measures to which our country is committed by existing laws, viz: resumption in specie, combined with demonetization of silver, are likely, if attempted to be enforced, to end in distress and defeat.

Fourth. Therefore, one of these measures will have to be abandoned, and that one is the demonetization of silver. In other words, we shall have to restore the double standard of gold and silver which existed from 1792 to 1873.

Fifth. I next review the relative value of gold and silver from the earliest times to the present, and show how constant that relation has been, particularly since the discovery of America and the opening of the East India and China trades, since which time and up to 1873 it scarcely varied from its pivotal point of 15½ to 1. The sources of this long-continued constancy of relation are then examined, and in their nature is found strong assurance that the relation will continue to be constant in the future.

Sixth. The principal and almost only cause of aberration in this relation is found to be the various edicts or enactments which in various countries and at various times have interfered with the freedom of money. Prominent among these were the Demonetization of silver in England in 1816, the Monetary Treaty of the Five Powers in 1865, the Demonetization Act of the United States in 1873, and the pending measures of the German Government. These various measures are adverted to and condemned as mischievous interferences with trade.

Seventh. The impracticability of abolishing the double standard is greatly strengthened by reference to the annual supplies of gold and silver separately since the beginning of the present century. From this reference it appears that the supplies of gold to the world have fluctuated between $5,000,000 and $182,000,000 per annum, that the supply has been diminishing since 1852, and that it is at the present time insufficient to meet the demands of the world for that metal for use in the arts and to keep good the wear and loss of coin. On the other hand the annual supplies of silver have always been steady, and are now but little above the average. Moreover gold is shown to be essentially a British product, while silver is essentially American.

Eighth. I then propose to show the impossibility of resuming specie payments in gold, the disadvantages and danger of attempting to demonetize silver, the impracticability of demonetizing it permanently, and to discuss the various objections that have been urged against remonetization.

Ninth. I shall also endeavor to show that the effect of remonetizing silver, or rehabilitating the double standard, will be to equalize more nearly the values of the metals, so as to restore or tend to restore the relation that has hitherto, up to within a late date, existed between them for three centuries, and to afford a great impetus to the industrial and commercial prosperity of this country.

Tenth. I shall next endeavor to show that both gold and silver together at a relation fixed by law is the Constitutional money of this country, and that all acts of legislation intended to subvert this institution are illegal and void.

Eleventh, and finally. I will quote the authority of the most eminent legislators and publicists in favor of the double standard.

THE FUNCTION OF MONEY.

Money has been fitly described as an instrument designed to equitably measure commodities and services, with the view to effect their exchange, either at present or in the future, and throughout the world. This is its specific function, and it has no other. The money of the world, at the present time, the substance in which prices are quoted, contracts made, and debts lawfully paid, consists of gold and silver coins; in most countries, silver coins alone; in many countries, both gold and silver coins, at a relation of weight and value fixed by law as nearly as possible to the market or commercial relation; in a few countries gold coins alone. In some countries some form of paper notes, either representing or promising to pay one or both of the precious metals, are employed at intervals as convenient substitutes, or temporary expedients, for money. In some countries silver tokens or partly representative coins; and in all countries tokens of copper, bronze, or other inferior metals, are employed for small payments. The preference for silver and gold for money is the result of thirty centuries of every conceivable sort of experiment to obviate the use of the precious metals, and for this reason, it is deemed hardly necessary in this place to advert more particularly to the numerous and well-marked characteristics which have procured for the precious metals this high preferment. Briefly, these are:

1. Eligibility of voluntary interchange into and with other forms of capital. This is the first and most necessary characteristic of money, the one without which it must prove useless. If its interchangeability instead of being voluntary is merely sustained by law, the money cannot equitably measure future exchanges, for human law is mutable and subject to vicissitude, alteration, and overthrow. If its interchangeability is costly, as it would be if the money were made of iron or cotton, the money would be of inferior eligibility to money made of the precious metals, which are easily and cheaply convertible from coins into plate and other forms of capital, and from these forms into coins.

This quality of voluntary and economical interchangeability furnishes constant security to the holder of gold and silver money: a security which no act of legal tender can enhance. Money possessing this and the other characteristics hereafter named needs no law to make it current throughout the world. It is these characteristics which alone can give it currency; not the force of law, which is only the force of one nation at one time and as modified by the defects of administration and the friction of evasion. Since the arts of smelting and refining iron and the other more common and now more useful metals, and of making china and glass, were discovered and perfected, the forms of capital into which the precious metals can be economically converted are perhaps less numerous or important than formerly, many of the materials or instruments of reproduction or ornamentation which are now made of iron, glass, etc., having been formerly made of the precious metals; for example, saddlery-hardware, buttons, buckles, thimbles, bells, lamps, goblets, plates, ewers, basins, etc. Nevertheless the use of the precious metals for these and other and newer purposes, whence they are readily converted into coin, is still very important, as *e. g.* watchmaking, plate and plated ware, jewelry, regalia, pens, dentistry, etc. They are, also, largely employed in photography, sign-painting, bookbinding, printing, medals, etc.

The security thus afforded to the owner of gold and silver money is not merely confined to an assurance that he may obtain for it at the present time and anywhere a full equivalent for the commodities or services it costs; it extends that assurance, or the nearest possible approximation to it, over all time. The cheap convertibility of such money into other and numerous forms of usefulness is a check against the heaping up of such money; the cheap convertibility of plate, and many of the other forms into which the precious metals are usually cast, is a check against the depletion of such money. The relation between the supply and demand for the precious metals is by no means a constant one as to either or both metals; this relation varies, but the variation is less, and is spread over longer periods of time than is the case with any other commodity. Did the precious metals possess no other advantage over other commodities which might be suggested as useful for money, this one of minimum variability, alone, would be sufficient to render them pre-eminently fitted for that purpose.

2. Adequateness and steadiness of supply to the world. These characteristics are shared with the precious metals by many other commodities or instruments capable, or supposed to be capable, of measuring present and future values. On the other hand, there are others which do not share it, as, the principal articles of food, clothing, and shelter, whose inadequacy and unsteadiness are proved by the limits which their supply puts upon population; it having been demonstrated that population would double in at least every twenty-five years, did the supply of the means of subsistence permit. Even the precious metals themselves have sometimes failed of adequate or steady supply, and never without occasioning the direst calamities; but the danger is less with them than with any other commodities known to man, both because of their profuse and diffused distribution in the earth and of their lasting qualities when produced.

3. Diffusion of supply and consumption throughout the world and ease of recovery. The precious metals are found in all countries and used in all countries for purposes other than money. The diffusion of their supply and consumption is greater than that of any other commodities. In some countries there is no iron, in others no cotton, in others no wool, in others no grain can be grown or cattle raised, and even in many countries where iron is found there is no fuel for smelting it. The competition in smelting causes it to be essentially a monopoly in countries possessing the cheapest fuel. Similar considerations affect all commodities, but gold and silver the least. These metals are often found in a pure state, and were obtained in the early ages of mankind with the aid of a flint-chisel and sometimes even with the fangs of a boar.* It is within the power of the humblest and most solitary adventurer to extract, refine, and coin these metals, processes which can be pursued with the other metals only by the help of co-operation and capital. The supply of the money of the world must be a monopoly to no country and to no class of men; otherwise the fortunes of all the rest might stand in imminent jeopardy from those who monopolized it.

4. Exemption from decay. The precious metals will neither decay, corrode, oxydize, nor evaporate. They resist not only the atmosphere, but the strongest acids. There is still extant a legible specimen of gold coins issued in Ionia about nine centuries before Christ.† There was a legible stamped gold coin in the Earl of Pembroke's collection which was issued by Darius, of Persia, about 480 years before Christ.* The gold coins of Alexander the Great, about 330 B. C., which have never been excelled in purity of metal or boldness and beauty of design, are still so abundant that collectors regard them as less rare than any American gold piece of the last century.§ There are legible silver coins still circulating in England which were issued by the governments of ancient Rome.||

---

*Jacob, 17. †App. Cyc., 12, p. 443. §App. Cyc., 12, p. 444. ||McLeod.

In times of war and civil commotion, when the solemn earth becomes the womb of man's rehabilitation, as it had once been that of his existence, and is always that of his support, the quality of exemption from decay of the precious metals is not the least valuable one, nor are these the only times when such a characteristic proves valuable. Accidents from fire, water, and many other causes are continually happening to destroy man's possessions; but the precious metals survive them all.

5. The two precious metals are naturally complementary to each other. Hitherto the precious metals have been mentioned together, and the advantages ascribed to them attributed to both. This is quite correct if both be taken together, but not entirely so if either metal is taken singly. Some countries which produce gold do not produce silver; as Great Britain and its colonies. Others produce more silver than gold, as the United States, Mexico, and the South American States. In others, again, the gold and silver occur in the same matrix, as in the Comstock lode. Some countries consume little or no gold; others little or no silver. Hence the distribution of supply and demand varies; so does its steadiness. During certain periods of time the world's current supply, as compared with its current consumption, of silver, outruns that of gold, as it did from the beginning to nearly the middle of this century. During other periods gold outruns silver, as from about the year 1837 to 1870. Thus, taken separately, the precious metals do not exhibit those advantages which they possess together. Moreover, in many countries, the use of both metals for money is rendered necessary by reason of their very different value as compared with bulk or weight. These considerations will be alluded to again; they are only mentioned in this place in order to justify the employment of the dual term precious metals, and to account for their forming together the money of the world.

6. The superior ductility and malleability of the precious metals is one of the most important of their characteristics, for it renders the cost of manufacturing coins so

small, as practically to entail no loss upon the owners in case it became desirable to reduce them to bars. This is always the case when legal enactments place a false or mistaken value (as respects commodities or services already sold, or contracted to be sold in future) upon the coins. The comparative cheapness and ease of transforming the coins into bars, in which form the metal is certain to command its true market value, affords a continual check upon legislation and defeats its every attempt to misvalue coins. Metals possessing inferior ductility are lacking in this advantage, the cost of making them into coins and the loss by reducing them to bars proving an obstacle to their quick and ready transmutation. Substances other than metals do not possess this characteristic at all. The cost of manufacturing coins is called brassage, and is about ½ of 1 per cent. In some countries another and wholly indefensible charge, in addition to this, is imposed. It is called seigniorage, and consists of brassage and a profit. This profit is a royal prerogative, and, as its name indicates, is a relic of the feudal ages of medieval Europe.

There are other well marked characteristics which render the precious metals superior to all other instruments or services susceptible of being employed to measure values. The homogeneity of these substances renders their genuineness and purity easy to test and difficult to counterfeit or impair; enables all bodies of them, however large or small, easy to divide or unite, and without adding to, or diminishing, the labor or service which they represent. They are easier to transport and conceal, less liable to abrasion, and, being inodorous, are less offensive to handle than other substances.

It is difficult to estimate what relation the cost of this instrument bears to that of the commodities and services it measures, because the commerce of the world is carried on largely by means of paper instruments, some of which are indeed based upon the metals and merely represent them, while others are based upon private or corporative credit, and still others on no credit at all but mere force of law. There is another difficulty in making such a calculation: that which arises from the well-known fact that a vast number of the largest transactions consist of stock-jobbing, or mere bets clothed in the garb of business operations. Making a reasonable allowance for these facts, it has been calculated that specie measures ten thousand times its own value every year, and that taking gold and silver together in the actual proportions in which they exist in the currencies of the world, specie will last, as against abrasion, loss by accident, &c., about a thousand years.* Upon this basis the actual cost of this instrument is an infinitessimal charge upon each transaction, probably as little as that caused by the wear and tear of any other measure, as a tape-line, a pint-pot, a bushel-basket, &c.

On the other hand, money made of the precious metals has several defects. It is somewhat costly to produce, it is somewhat expensive to transport. It is always a misfortune to society, as well as to the individual, when specie is lost at sea, or buried in hoards the secret of which does not transpire. It is subject to loss from abrasion, it fluctuates in value, and the two metals fluctuate unevenly.

Some of these defects have been remedied by the invention of expedients. Transportation and loss are measurably obviated by bills of exchange and places and certificates of deposit; abrasion is lessened by the use of alloy in coins; the uneven fluctuation of the two metals is remedied by a double standard, which, by fixing a mean relation covering a long period of time, past and prospective, enables both metals at that relation to be employed all the time.

There remain two other defects: the first cost of the precious metals and their fluctuating value as a duality even after such fluctuation has been lessened by using them together. These defects are extremely small and

---

*According to Jacob, the stock of coin in Europe at the beginning of the present era received little or no addition until the Discovery of America. This was a period of fifteen hundred years, during which the stock dwindled down to little more than ten per cent. of its original dimensions.

are of a nature which renders them unavoidable by any safe or practicable means.

Let us begin with the question of cost. Present and future values cannot be equitably or nearly equitably measured by anything that is not capable of being voluntarily and readily interchanged with other forms of capital; in a word, by anything that of itself does not contain or represent an amount of labor or service easy to determine, and of a kind appreciable to and exchangeable with all mankind.

Value, which is not to be confused with either worth, utility, or desirability, is the quantitative relation between two services exchanged.* This relation can only arise in the social state; whilst worth, utility, and desirability are qualities appreciable to the isolated man as well as to society. Value is not a quality inherent in a service; as worth, utility, and desirability are; it is simply a relation between two services exchanged.

A measure of value must therefore be a service of some sort, and the more universally such service is appreciated the better measure will it afford. An abstraction, as an imaginary money of account or an irredeemable credit, cannot measure the quantitative relation between two services, and hence cannot be a measure of value.

There is an easy method of testing this assertion. Repeal the promise of payment which now causes treasury notes to usurp the place of specie, and observe what kind of money will continue current and what not. It will then be seen that the precious metals will circulate as before without the least abatement, indeed, with a slight enhancement of their purchasing power. This, indeed, is the case in China, a country which tried fiat currency six hundred years ago, but in which, in spite of the fact that there are now neither legal tender nor coinage laws, gold and silver both circulate at even a higher value than in countries where such laws are in full force and effect.

If the impracticability of employing irredeemable credit

---

* Bastiat, Harmonies Polit. Econ, pp. 108–9.

for the purpose of money be admitted, and it is still claimed that some form of redeemable credit, as national, or bank, or individual notes, may with advantage be used as money in order to save the cost of the precious metals, the claim is admitted. There is and can be no objection to the use of such credit, so long as its use, like that of the Scotch bank notes, is entirely voluntary. The moment that legislation or any arbitrary act interferes to place it above this level, its use is fraught with danger. The advantage to be gained, which is merely that of saving the cost of the precious metals in a currency of safe and universally acceptable material, is wholly inadequate to the risk run. And on this point it is never to be lost sight of that so long as we continue to be, as we are, one of the principal producers of the precious metals, we lower to a small extent the value and selling price of all the metal we may have to export, by every expedient, the effect of which is to throw it out of employment in our own country.

In saying this, it is not intended to deny the advantage of employing credit as a convenient and economical medium of exchange; but such credit must rest upon so firm and broad a foundation of the precious metals as not to need the aid of legislation to prop it up. In other words, its use must rest upon the same foundation as the use of the precious metals themselves—common and voluntary consent.

As to the other unavoidable defect of money made of the precious metals, its fluctuating value, it can only be replied that this fluctuation is exceedingly slow. That is all the defense of it there is, and there can be no better one, for all measures of value must fluctuate, though none of them less than the precious metals. There are men who have imagined an absolute and fixed measure of value, as there have been others who imagined a fixed earth or a fixed sun, an absolute or unconditioned quality or quantity, etc. To such men it need only be replied that there is nothing fixed or absolute; nothing, at least, that the senses of man can perceive or his mind imagine. All is in motion, all is conditioned. The universe and all it contains is incessantly in action, and even the adjectives of language which are employed to qualify or characterize the objects brought to our conception, are themselves relative and conditioned. A fixed measure of value is an inconceivability; we can but prefer for such a measure the commodities or services which fluctuate in value the least, and these are the precious metals.

This brief exposition of the functions and characteristics of money may be still more briefly summarised as follows:

1. Money is an instrument voluntarily adopted to equitably measure values, present and future.

2. Value is the relation between two commodities or services exchanged.

3. Hence money is the measure of the relation between commodities and services exchanged.

4. This measure is formed most conveniently and equitably of both the precious metals taken together.

5. Legislation cannot make or unmake money. It may temporarily exalt or depress the value of one metal as against the other, but only temporarily; it may disturb, but it cannot permanently alter or destroy. Gold and silver are money in virtue of their own superiority, and they owe none of their rank to law.

The extent to which legislation can be beneficially exercised with regard to money is to quantitatively define the names of coins, to guard against confusion, counterfeiting, etc., by manufacturing them in a public mint, and to save the transportation and abrasion of them by receiving them on deposit and issuing certificates therefor.*

To insure the fourth provision, that both the precious metals shall form the ingredients of money, it is essential that no legal obstacle shall be placed in the way of the voluntary use of either; that one, equally with the other, shall be a legal tender to an unlimited amount, at a quantitative relation fixed from time to time in view of the past

---

*Herbert Spencer, in N. Y. Social Science Review, p. 137.

and probable future market ratio of these metals. To these must be added copper tokens for petty sums, and upon the whole will naturally arise a paper credit peculiar to each country; a credit whose volume will regulate itself in view of the basis beneath it, in view of its command of the precious metals, in view of the wants of industry and of the conditions of security which exist within the social or political organization to which it belongs.

These are the essential principles of money which seem to be deducible from the united testimony of history, experience, and reflection. When we come to apply these principles to any existing monetary system not in accordance with them, as is the case with that of this country, we are in the position of a physician who, believing himself to be acquainted with the laws of health, may nevertheless be puzzled how to prescribe for a given case of disease. Happily I have no such task before me. My single object is to remove an impediment to recovery, an impediment the nature and importance of which, will, I believe, be recognized as promptly by those who may differ with me as to what are the true principles of money, as by those who may agree with me in regard to those principles. The removal of this impediment, while it will afford that ease which one school of currency demands, nevertheless affords it entirely within the scope of action which the other school prescribes. It simply proposes the re-establishment of the double standard, unwisely abolished by the act of 1873, a piece of legislation whose evil effects can only be estimated by referring to that history of money from which I have ventured for a few moments to digress.

These views are not merely those of the ablest men who have devoted their attention to the subject; they are gathered from the history of money from the time when this instrument was first known to mankind, to the present. They are enforced not only by precept, but by example; they are written in the rise and fall of States and of social systems, in revolutions, in wars, in the annals of freedom and in those of feudalism and slavery. They are imprinted in sweat, and tears, and blood; and to disregard them is to disregard the lessons of thirty centuries of time.

The use of gold and silver for money is not a recent one, neither were these costly metals adopted for the purpose until after every other expedient practicable at the time had been tried. The following table furnishes a list of these expedients and other chronological data in reference to money:

Table showing some of the Substances which have at various periods and in various countries been used as Money.

PERIOD.	COUNTRY.	SUBSTANCE USED AS MONEY.	AUTHORITY.
B. C.			
1900	Palestine.	Cattle; and gold and silver by w't.	The Scriptures.
——	Arabia.	Gold and silver coins.	Jacob.
——	Phœnicia.	Gold, silver and copper coins.	Anonymous.
——	Phœnician colony in Spain.	Same, (some still extant.)	Carter.
1200	Phrygia.	Coins by Queen of Pelops.	Julius Pollux.
1184	Greece.	Brass coins.	Homer,
862	Argos.	Gold and silver coins by Phidon.	Dic. of Dates.
700–500	Rome.	Brass by weight.	Jacob.
578	Rome.	Copper coins.	Ibid.
Uncertain.	Carthage.	Leather or parchment money, first "paper bills" known.	Socrates, Dial. on Riches, Journ'l des Economistes, 1874, p. 354.
491	Sicily.	Gold coins by Gelo, (some still extant.)	Jacob.
480	Persia.	Gold coins by Darius, (two still extant.)	Ibid.
478	Sicily.	Gold coins by Hiero, (some still extant.)	Ibid.
407	Athens.	Debased gold coins, foreign.	McLeod, 476.
400	Sparta.	Iron, over valued.	Bœckh.
360	Macedonia.	First gold coins coined in Greece by Phillip.	Jacob.
266	Rome.	First silver coins coined in Rome.	Ibid.
54	Britain.	Pieces of iron.	Ibid.
50	Rome.	Tin and brass coins.	Dic. of Dates.
Uncertain.	Arabia.	Glass coins.	N. Y. Tribune, July 2, 1872.
A. D.	*Period following the failure of the ancient mines.*		
212	Rome. (Caracalla.)	Lead coins silvered and copper coins gilded.	Anonymous.
1066	Britain.	Living money, or human beings made a legal tender for debts at about £2 16*s*. 3*d*., *per capita.*	Henry's History of Great Britain, vol. iv, p. 243.
	Period of representatives for money.		
1160	Italy.	Paper invented; bills of exchange introduced by the Jews.	Anderson.
1240	Milan, Italy.	Paper bills a legal tender.	Arthur Young.
1275	China.	Paper bills a legal tender.	Marco Polo.
——	Africa, part of	"Machutes" or "ideal money." This view doubted.	Montesquieu.
1470	Grenada, Spain.	Paper bills a legal tender.	Irving.
1574	Holland.	Pasteboard bills, representative.	Dic. of Dates.
Uncertain.	Iceland.	Dried fish.	Anonymous.
Uncertain.	Newfoundland.	Codfish, dried.	Anonymous.
Uncertain.	Norway and Greenland.	Seal skins and blubber.	Anonymous.

Table—Continued.

PERIOD.	COUNTRY.	SUBSTANCE USED AS MONEY.	AUTHORITY.
Uncertain.	Hindostan and parts of Africa.	Cowrie shells.	Jacob, 372.
Uncertain.	North America, Indian Tribes.	Agate, cornelian, jasper, lead, copper, gold, silver, terra-cotta, mica, pearl, lignite, coal, bone, shells, chalcedony, wampumpeag, etc.	Anonymous.
Uncertain.	Oriental pastoral tribes.	Cattle, grain, etc.	Anonymous.
Uncertain.	Abyssinia.	Salt.	Anonymous.
Uncertain.	China and India.	Rice.	Anonymous.
Uncertain.	India.	Paper bills.	Patterson, p, 13.
Uncertain.	China.	Pieces of silk cloth.	Ibid.
Uncertain.	Africa.	Strips of cotton cloth.	Ibid.
	Not stated.	Wooden tallies or checks.	Ibid.
A. D.	*Period following the discovery of the American mines.*		
1631	Massachusetts.	Corn a legal tender at market prices.	Macgreggor.
1635	Massachusetts.	Musket balls.	Anonymous.
1690	Massachusetts	Paper bills, colonial notes.	Macgreggor.
1694	England.	Bank notes.	McCulloch.
1700	Sweden.	Copper and iron coins.	Voltaire's "Charles XII."
1702	South Carolina.	Colonial notes.	Macgreggor.
1712	South Carolina.	Bank notes.	Ibid.
1716	France.	Inter-convertible paper bills a legal tender.	Murray.
1723	Pennsylvania.	Paper bills, colonial notes.	Macgreggor.
1732	Maryland.	Indian corn a legal tender at 23*d.* per bushel.	Anonymous.
1732	Maryland.	Tobacco a legal tender at 1*d.* per pound.	Anonymous.
1776	Scotland.	Tenpenny nails for small change.	Adam Smith.
1785	Frankland, State of, (now part of North Car.)	Linen at 3*s.* 6*d.* per yard, whisky at 2*s.* 6*d.* per gallon, and peltry as legal tenders.	Wheeler's History of North Carolina, 94.
	Period following the failure of the American mines.		
1810–1840	All commercial countries.	Great era of bank paper bills.	-
1826	Russia.	Platinum coins, (discontinued in 1845.)	App. Encyc.
1847	Mexico, parts of.	Cocoa beans, and at Castle of Perote, soap.	Anonymous.
	Period following the openings of California and Australia.		
1849	California.	Gold dust by weight, also minute gold coins for small change coined in private mints.	-
1855	Australia.	Gold dust by weight.	-
185–	Communist settlement in Ohio called "Utopia."	Paper bills each representing "one hour's labor."	Private information.
	Period following the suspension of specie payments in the United States.		
1862	United States.	Paper bills a legal tender.	Act of Feb. 25.
1863	North Carolina.	Tenpenny nails, at 5 cents each, for small change.	Anonymous.
1863	Camp at Florence, South Carolina.	Potatoes for small change.	Yorkville Enquirer.
1863	United States.	Postage stamps for small change, temporary.	-
1865	Philadelphia. Pa.	Turnips for small change, temporary and local.	Philadel. Ledger, April.
1865	United States.	Nickel coins for small change, overvalued.	Act of March 3.

It will be observed that the commodities selected to serve the purpose of money during those early ages when the countries of the world were not connected by commerce were always those of adequate, steady, and diffused supply, and, therefore, of most common acceptation in each country. Thus, in forestal ages, the skins of wild animals were usually employed; in pastoral ages, cattle; * in early agricultural ages, grain; in early mining ages, base metal; in early manufacturing ages, glass, musket-balls, nails, strips of cotton, etc.

The significance of this deduction will not fail to be appreciated. After commerce had connected various countries, substances common to all countries, viz: the precious metals, were found to be necessary for the purpose of money, and later still, balances of trade were settled by means of bills of exchange representing those metals; and it is worthy of remark that gold and silver are the only substances which have ever been universally used for money.

Development from the early agricultural to the mining, manufacturing, and commercial ages indicates not only a development of occupation, but also a development of political organization. The hunter, the shepherd, the early agriculturist, needed neither social oganization nor government. He could prosecute his occupations alone; and in these stages of development mankind lived in isolated families or small tribes of freemen. The progress of agriculture and of mining, which must have followed agriculture,† of manufacturing and of commerce, rendered fixed residences and division of labor necessary, and the protection of the one and regulation of the other demanded the offices of government. The hunter and shepherd could defend himself and his possessions or convey them out of

---

* *Shekel*, a lamb; *pecus*, (whence pecunia, pecuniary, etc.,) cattle; *feoh*, (whence fee, Saxon, German, etc.,) cattle.

† Mining doubtless originated in that upturning of the soil which occurs in the pursuit of agriculture. Indeed, history affords an instance of the kind. "In Pæonia the husbandman, while plowing, found pieces of gold." Strabo, VII, (Chrestom,) p. 331, as quoted in Bœckh, p. 10.

the reach of enemies; the agriculturist, miner, manufacturer and merchant, needed the protection of a military force and the security of well-executed laws.

Following the local or feudal powers which sprang into existence to meet these demands, came also those abuses, which always, sooner or later, accompany the exercise of power.

The warrior classes reduced the working classes to a condition of predial servitude, and those who at first were mere chieftains of choice became arbitrary and despotic lords paramount. Not least among the powers which they abused were those relating to the coinage and denomination of the precious metals.

Up to this period in the history of countries it is to be remarked that, whatever substance came to be employed for money in each country, whether, as at first, the peculiar and most common product of each respective country, or, as afterward, those substances more or less common to all countries and most convenient everywhere, viz., the precious metals, such substance was employed, as it is now in China, without command or force of law. The importance of this fact cannot be overestimated, for its recognition must ever form the basis of all sound legislation upon this subject. The precious metals do indeed, no doubt, derive some small element of their purchasing power from the fact that now all governments provide that, when coined in a certain way, they shall be a legal tender for the payment of debts; but this element of value is very small and probably does not exceed the seigniorage or charge for coinage. Whatever it may be, it is so small that there can be no risk in asserting that, were all the legal tender laws of the world repealed to-day and forever, neither gold nor silver would lose an appreciable atom of their power to purchase present commodities, secure future contracts, or pay past debts. Indeed, with the example of China before us, an example which in this respect at least is not without utility, it is believed to be more than probable that their purchasing power would increase; for setting aside the effect of such repeal upon the continuance of unrepresentative paper notes, it would dissipate the very considerable fears that now attach themselves to every contract, wherein the words dollar, pound, or franc are employed to express a given weight of metal.

It has been stated that with the growth of governmental power came abuses in coinage and the denomination of coins. These abuses, like all others, were of gradual growth. The power and authority of feudal lords and monarchs were first employed in this respect beneficially, and government was exercised within its proper scope, Local, separated, and diverse systems of weights and measures, and of the weights and measures of gold and silver pieces, gave way to national, united, and uniform systems. Isolated and anomalous measures of values, adopted in small localities for greater temporary convenience—as pieces of iron in Africa and Sparta and of glass in some parts of Arabia—were prohibited by legal tender laws; for so long as they were suffered to exist, they promoted provincial isolation and defeated national homogeneity and political unity. The same laws also provided in what substances debts were to be paid in cases unadjudicatable either by express stipulation or common usage.

In these early ages. while men yet retained the power to resist misgovernment, the names attached to pieces of the precious metals were always those of the weights contained in such pieces, as the Jewish shekel, of nearly one-half of an ounce Troy; the Attic drachma, of little more than one-fourth of an ounce Troy, etc.

To prevent counterfeiting* and economize time, and thus facilitate exchanges, these pieces of metal were ordered to be coined, and governments monopolized, as governments do still, the function of coining. To the coins thus manufactured were given the names of their weights, and thus far the laws regulating the coinage of the precious metals were honestly conceived and probably as honestly executed.

With the lapse of time, however, coupled with use of

---

*False gold coins from Samos were successfully passed in Sparta so early as B. C. 540. (Bœckh, 33.)

coins and the increasing power of authority, abuses crept into the coinage which have lasted to this day. The names of coins, which at first were literal weights, came, for convenience' sake, to be used as symbols; and men no longer bargained for so much gold or silver as would weigh a shekel or a drachma, but for so many shekels or drachmas "current with the merchant." In this state of affairs the temptation on the part of rulers and the classes who environ power to commit abuses became too strong for resistance.

Owing to the frequency of the practice of degrading and debasing the coins, in all countries and ages, the quantitative meaning attached to the names of coins has been so often changed that, to interpret these names or the sums of money mentioned in them, in ancient or medieval historical works, into modern weights, is almost an unsafe proceeding, even in the hands of professional metrologists.*

In order to deceptively reduce the pay of the army, what more easy method offered itself to a ruler than that of diminishing by decree and recoinage the weight of pure metal in the "drachma." * In order, at other times, to exact greater fees or subsidies, what more easy expedient suggested itself to a feudal lord than to increase the weight of the "drachma?" † In cases where the ruler was not unscrupulous enough to tamper with the coin for his own profit, there were never wanting powerful classes of men, both ecclesiastical and secular, to urge him to similar practices for their advantage. Though instances occur in history where the standard was restored after the coins had been debased, the general course of affairs was in the opposite direction—a fact due to the inability of the government to redeem the debased coin.‡

---

*The "dollar" of a few grains weight was formerly the "thaler" of more than an ounce, and anciently the "talent" of many pounds.

†See instance of Lord King's exaction of his tenants' rents in gold during the bank suspension. (MacLeod's Dictionary Polit. Econ., i, 98.)

‡The gold scriptulum was debased in Rome so early as B. C. 207. Bœckh, 44.)

I do not propose at this time to enter any further into the history of these events; my object thus far having been merely to show that money, in the early ages, whatever it was made of, came into use voluntarily; was always composed of substances of supposed adequate and steady supply; owed none of its utility to legal-tender laws, which were originally enacted for other and more practicable purposes; and, up to the period of the dark ages in Europe, had consisted for at least three thousand years of gold and silver coins only.

We have now to consider three other points in this connection: the World's supply and consumption of the precious metals, the effects of an inadequate or monopolized supply, and the necessity of adhering to both of the precious metals for the basis of a national currency, whether the same shall consist wholly of the precious metals or partly of convertible paper credits, or representative money.

HISTORY OF THE SUPPLY AND CONSUMPTION OF THE PRECIOUS METALS IN EUROPE.

The repeated destructions of historical works previous to the invention of paper, and the subsequent one of printing, have left us but little exact information on this subject. We only know generally that previous to the Macedonian Empire both of the precious metals were comparatively common in farther Asia* and scarce in Europe. This much we gather from the sizes of the pieces that were coined and used for circulating money in the respective regions,

*There is an instance in Strabo's 16th book of an eastern country, (possibly India,) bordering on that of the Sabaens, (Arabia?) where gold to silver was only 1 for 2, and to bronze only 1 for 3. With the instance before us of modern Japan, where gold (purity not stated) was quoted in 1853 at 1 to 4 of silver, it may seem bold to challenge this assertion, but other instances in regard to China assure us that Oriental quotations are unreliable, from the fact that in the early ages gold and silver ingots, impure and largely burdened with base substances, circulated as money, and the quoted relation referred to the value of these impure ingots, and not to the value of the pure metals. Consult a pam-

the prices of commodities and services, the enumeration of royal and princely treasures, and the employment of the precious metals in the arts. The relation of gold to silver in ancient and farther Asia has not been determined.

At a later period, about B. C. 500, we hear of it in Persia, at 1 to 13. After this period and on this point the annals of the Orient were closed for many centuries. At about the same period the relation of gold to silver in Europe was about 1 to 12.5. From this relation gold rose to 1 to 13½ and even 15, until the time of expeditions of Alexander the Great. These, through the influence of the vast treasures in gold of which they despoiled the eastern countries, brought gold down again to 1 to 10, at which rate it stood in the time of the comic poet Menander, about B. C. 300. That it was the fluctuations in the supply of gold, and not those of silver, which occasioned the most of these changes of relation, we are assured, from the sporadic influxes of gold alluded to, and from Xenophon's encomium on silver, written about B. C. 383; while Bœckh himself, in his work on *The Public Economy of the Athenians*, from which these details are gleaned, says, generally, that "the value of gold is more fluctuating than that of silver," and that "the latter, therefore, may be considered the scale for determining the price of gold, as well as of other commodities."*

After the Macedonian conquests the stock of the precious metals in Europe increased very rapidly until at about the beginning of our era, when, according to the estimate of Mr. Wm. Jacob, it amounted, throughout the Roman em-

---

phlet by "A Disciple of Franklin," in American Philosophical Society library, Philadelphia, No. 6332, page 9, where it is stated that Chinese gold from Sumatra, Celebes, &c., was but 16 to 18 carats fine, and that the relation in China in about the year 1810 was 1 in gold, *as thus found*, to 12 in (pure) silver. At least we can feel fully assured that the relations mentioned by Strabo were local, and only referred to the particular locality indicated. Consult Bœckh, p. 43. Another anomalous and still more extraordinary though possibly not unauthentic instance of the kind is related in Jacob's History Precious Metals, p. 57.

* Bœckh, 33.

pire, to a quantity equal in value to about $1,740,000,000 of the present time. The relative proportions of gold and silver are not calculated. The relation of value between the metals in the Roman empire was, about B. C. 207, 1 to 13.7, and about B. C., 50 or 64 years before the period of Jacob's estimate, 1 to 11.9.

From about the beginning of the Christian era to the present time the history of the precious metals has been traced very closely, and with great labor and acumen, by three great historians: Wm. Jacob, whose work covers the entire period from the year 14 to the year 1830; Baron Von Humboldt, whose work covers the period from the discovery of America until the early part of the present century; and Michel Chevalier, whose work brings the history up to within twenty years of the present time.

The salient points of this long though extremely interesting history are:

1. The separation of the Asian and European histories of money, from the downfall of the Roman military power until the Eastern trade was reopened in part by the medieval Italians and Arabians, and wholly by the Portuguese navigators; and, 2. The failure of the European mines previous to the downfall of Rome and the gradual decline of the stock of precious metals thenceforward until the ninth century; its stationary condition until the discovery of America; its rapid increase thereafter, until about the beginning of the present century; its subsequent temporary decline from the year 1809 to 1830; its slow increase thereafter; its rapid increase from the time when the effects of the opening of the Russian, American, and Australian mines were felt, until within late years; and its stationary condition at the present time.

Omitting from further mention all that is not necessary for the purposes of this review, let us briefly follow Mr. Jacob's history of the precious metals from the beginning of the Christian era.

From the enormous wealth of individuals, the high prices of commodities and services, the vast revenues of the State, and other circumstances, Mr. Jacob conjectured that, in the time of Augustus Cæsar, the quantity of money in existence in ancient Rome, which then substantially comprised the whole civilized world, was £358,000,000, or about $1,740,000,000 The correctness of this sum is deemed to be rendered the more probable from the fact that Vespasian, when afterward he succeeded to the imperial dignity, asserted that a sum equivalent to £322,916,600 was necessary to support the commonwealth—meaning, not the government, for neither the annual revenue nor the accumulation of the treasury, bore any proximate relation to this vast sum—but the nation at large. It is believed that he mentioned a sum which coincided, as far as is known, with the whole mass of coined money then believed to exist, and upon this supposition, and the inferences to which it leads, historical writers have hitherto been content to rest.

A few instances of the abundance of money at that period may not be out of place. Crassus possessed in lands *bis millies* (£1,615,000,) besides many slaves and furniture valued at much more. Seneca possessed *ter millies* (£2,420,-000;) Pallas an equal sum; Lentulus *quater millies* (£3,-230,000;) Augustus Cæsar obtained from private legacies *quater decies millies* (£32,300,000,) and Tiberius left at his death *vigesies acsepties millies* (£21,800,000,) which Caligula lavished away in a single year. Cæsar when he went to Spain was in debt £2,018,000, and Anthony squandered of the public money more than £5,600,000 sterling.

These facts were compiled by Jacob chiefly from Adams's Roman Antiquities, while the sterling sums were computed by Arbuthnot. I prefer to retain them as originally computed.

Augustus frequently gave *congiaria*, ranging from 4*s*. 10*d*. to £2 2*s* 1*d*. per head to the whole population, men, women, and children; and, at his death, left all the common men £2 8*s*. 5*d*. each. In this prodigious liberality he was even exceeded by several other emperors, but the instances demand too much space. Milo gave each voter a bribe of

£32 8*s.* 10*d.* Claudius promised each soldier for his vote £113, and Julian £210 16*s.* Otho promised to the attainers of Galba a reward of £403 12*s.* each, and paid them £80 14*s.* in advance, etc., etc.

In the time of Augustus the gold and silver mines which had kept good Rome's supply of treasure gave out and ceased to be worked. Moreover, there was no more spoil of the precious metals to be obtained in Asia or Northern Europe.

This was due to the exhaustion of those conquered countries, to the unsettled condition of the empire, to wars, the incursions of barbarians, the insufficiency of mechanical resources, the loss of life and hardships of the slaves employed in the mines, which induced them to desert their occupation whenever civil commotion afforded them a convenient opportunity, and to other causes set forth by our author.*

From that time, therefore, the stock of money decreased, and it has been calculated that the decrement proceeded at the following rate:

Year of the Christian era.	Stock of coin in civilized world.	Year of the Christian era.	Stock of coin in civilized world.
14	£358,000,000	446	£96,692,332
50	322,200,000	482	87,033,099
86	287,980,000	518	78,229,700
122	259,182,000	554	70,406,720
158	233,263,800	590	63,364,057
194	209,937,420	626	57,027,653
230	181,943,678	662	51,324,889
266	163,749,311	698	46,192,399
302	147,374,380	734	41,573,160
338	132,636,942	770	37,415,840
374	119,373,248	806	33,674,256
410	107,435,924		

A calculation so hypothetical as this must not, of course, be taken too literally. It is sufficient if its general correctness is supported by all the facts we know, and this

*An ancient law of the Roman senate actually forbade the Italian mines to be worked at all. Pliny, book iii, ch. 6, quoted in Jacob, 51.

seems to be the case. The gradually deepening misery of the populations of Europe during the medieval ages, the decay of the civil law, the demoralization of society, the disintegration of government and authority, the institution (probably reinstitution) of feudalism, the poverty, filth, pestilences, abominable crimes, ignorance, and wretchedness, that characterized this period of history and gave to it its well deserved name of the Dark Ages—these facts are too well known to need repeating. That such a condition of affairs was promoted solely by means of a gradual and constant diminution of the currency is not contended; though it would not be difficult to argue the result from the predicate. But that the diminution of the currency largely contributed to bring it about and maintain it, may be affirmed with entire confidence; and the careful thinker will find it difficult to discern a cause that will more satisfactorily account for that extraordinary breaking up of governments and arrest of social development and of the growth of population which occurred in Europe from about the beginning of the present era to the time of the discovery of America.

From the age of Augustus Cæsar to that of Charlemagne and the Saxon Heptarchy is like going from the mouth to the bottom of the ancient mines—above, all lightness, happiness, and life; below, all darkness, misery, and death.

These were the ages of alchemists and false coiners. They both sought to obtain gold from base metals; the first by transmutation, the other by arrant roguery. The base pieces they produced were known by the names of pollards, crocards, schuldings, brabants, eagles, leonines, sleepings, &c. Those who were pitched upon as the fabricators of these pieces were visited with fearful punishment. Racking, pressing to death, burning, drowning, and tramping were common enough. Whole families were exported, whole communities robbed and banished under the pretense of punishing coiners.

Such was the scarcity of the precious metals that *living money* was used instead. This consisted of *men and women*, who were thus passed from hand to hand as a legal tender.* The poverty and degradation of the people were inconceivable. The price of a hawk was the same as that of a man, and robbing the nest of one was as great a crime as depriving of life the other.† Famine and pestilence, superstition and tyranny, terror and outrage, reigned supreme.

These were the Dark Ages; and so profound were the depths into which they cast humanity that nearly a thousand years later Arthur Young thus quoted from the *cahiers* of the "tiers etat" of that feudal system to which the Middle Ages had given birth:

"Fixed and heavy rents; vexatious processes to secure them; appreciated unjustly to augment them; rents *solidaires* and *reveulbables;* rents, *cheantes*, and *levantes; fumages.* Fines at every change of the property, in the direct as well as collateral line; feudal redemption (*retraite*) fines on sale to the eighth and even the sixth penny (part;) redemptions (*rachats*) injurious in their origin, and still more so in their extension; *banalite* of the mill, of the oven, and of the cider-press; *corvees* by custom; *corvees* by usage of the fief; *corvees* established by unjust decrees; *corvees* arbitrary and even fantastical; servitudes; *prestations*, extravagant and burthensome; collections by assessments incollectible; *aveux, minus, impunissement;* litigations, ruinous and without end; the rod of seigneural finance forever shaken over our heads; vexation, ruin, outrage, violence, and distinctive servitude, under which the peasants, *almost on a level with Polish slaves*, can never but be miserable, vile, and oppressed."

Even the liberty to bruise between two stones a measure of barley was sold to these miserable creatures, while the names of the tortures to which they were subjected are eloquent in their very jargon and variety.

In order to preserve the game, in the pursuit of which the nobles trampled down the wretched crops and rode over the very bodies of the poor, there were numerous edicts, which prohibited weeding and hoeing, lest the young partridges should be disturbed; steeping seed, lest

* Henry's Hist. of Great Britain. † Jacob on Precious Metals, p. 170.

it should injure the game; manuring with night soil, lest the flavor of the partridges should be injured by feeding on the corn produced, &c.

Recollect that this was nearly a thousand years later than the period from which we have digressed, when, instead of tending downward, as it did until the middle of the twelfth century, society, under the combined influences of an increasing stock of coin, an increasing diffusion of wealth, and increasing industrial activity, was rapidly progressing towards liberty and affluence. Consider, then, what must have been the condition of affairs in the year 806; a period so unspeakably wretched that we have not even a contemporary account of its wretchedness!

Gold was nowhere to be had, and the few gold pieces in circulation were of an ancient Byzantine* coinage; whilst silver was so scarce, that, together with gold, it was at a subsequent period forbidden by an act of Henry V to be used in the arts.†

These instances could be multiplied almost indefinitely, but it is not necessary. It is sufficient if they attest the poverty, wretchedness and tyranny that attends a decline in the quantity of money or of the only bases upon which any system of money, representative or partly representative, can stand—the precious metals.

I am aware that the reply to this implication may be that it makes no difference how much the stock of coin is, if its only function is to measure value which is merely a relation. This position I admit to be well taken if the stock of money remains forever stationary, or, rather stationary *per capita* of population. In such case a grain of silver will measure quite as effectually the relation between a day's work and its equivalent in commodities, as a pound of silver will, with a stock of coin 5,760 times as great, and if money was already not concentrated in a few hands and there were no debts. The only limitation to the perfect equality of these two conditions of affairs would be that

---

*Jacob, 169. †*Ibid.*, 167.

in the one case coins might have to be made too small for convenient handling, or in the other too large.

But in point of fact there is not and never can be a continuously stationary amount of money in existence or even a stationary amount *per capita*. Money, as related to population, has a natural tendency to increase in quantity, because increase of money quickens industry and distributes wealth. Opposed to this tendency are wars, the failure of mines, the abrasion and loss of the precious metals, the insufficiency of mechanical resources, and the influence of wealthy classes. We have seen to what an appalling strait the first three of these causes brought, or assisted to bring, the European world—a strait in which it remained for nine hundred years; until it was freed by the discovery of the mines of Potosi. We shall yet see how the fourth cause operated at about the beginning of this century, and how the fifth cause is operating now.

These opposing tendencies, operating with varying force, alternately diminish and increase the stock of precious metals and place the subject quite beyond the category of fixed things. There is nothing fixed about it, and legislation must deal with it with all its eyes and ears opened. Left to itself and the industry and self-seeking of mankind, money would increase as all other commodities increase, and society would rapidly undergo that equalization of wealth which the vagaries of fortune would stamp with equity; but reduced to an unwilling wardship by monarchs and legislatures, dragged hither and thither at the nod of plutocrats, legal-tendered, single-standarded, royaltied, taxed, and bedeviled in every imaginable manner, it has been restrained and dwarfed in its increase, and made to become the instrument of half the misrule and misery which the world has undergone.

Though there was no increase in the European world's stock of coin from the beginning of the ninth century until the discovery of America, nevertheless there was no diminution. This arrest in the shrinkage of money is due to the invention, or, more probably, the reinvention of Bills of Exchange, which served to quicken money and enable a limited stock to perform the work of a large one.

The bill of exchange was unknown to the ancient Greeks and Romans. They were even without the use of paper upon which to inscribe these instruments. Obligations of debt even so late as the time of the Roman Empire having been inscribed upon tablets of wax; the limited supply of parchment being reserved for the higher purposes of literature. Paper was made in China so early as the second century before Christ, at about which time papyrus was invented in Egypt and parchment in Europe.

It is difficult to conceive of a great commercial nation—and there certainly was such an one at the time mentioned—having the use of paper and ignorant of the device known as bills of exchange. Be this as it may, an instrument known as the *hoondee*, and corresponding precisely with the modern bill of exchange, was known in India at a very early date; and the Hebrews, always a trading race, who were among the first to trade with India, "by Tadmor in the desert," very likely learned its use from that country.

These historical conjectures are, however, of little practical value in this connection. The material point is, that no sooner was paper invented or introduced into Europe, and possibly a little before,* than bills of exchange came into use, and that these events correspond with the time of lowest diminution in the stock of coin in Europe.

It has been suggested by some writers that the invention or introduction into Europe of the bill of exchange is due less to the ingenuity of the Jews or the art of making paper than to that improvement in social organizations and extension of political authority which distinguished the Italian republics of the medieval ages. To this suggestion it need only be repeated that bills of exchange were unknown to the Greek and Roman civilizations, and that,

---

*Some authors (*e. g.* Putnam's Cyclopedia) date the bill of exchange in Europe as far back as the year 808; others (*e. g.* Anderson in his Hist. Com.) date it, with greater probability, in A. D. 1160.

long after they came into use, their use was confined to the Jews; who, whatever may have been their confidence in medieval society, and medieval justice and political security, took great care never to trust to them, and traded chiefly with each other.

Following the introduction of bills of exchange came the establishment of those great Fairs, which for ages performed the functions of so many clearing-houses for the inland commerce of Europe; and next the establishment of banks in Italy, Spain, and Holland. The first fair dates from the year 886; the first bank, from which, however, no circulating notes were issued, was that of Venice, in 1167. These dates are oases in a desert of wretchedness and gloom.

But by far the most important of the several methods of relief which society so eagerly sought in this long era of money dearth was that adopted in Milan A. D. 1240, this being the year in which, according to Arthur Young,* paper circulating notes were first used in Europe. From the fact that at about the same time, or within a few years afterward, paper notes of the same character were employed in China,† there is some ground for the belief that the dearth of money in Europe was felt also in that distant and almost unconnected part of the world. In both these instances the notes used were issued by Government, and made a legal tender for the payment of debts.

Severe bullionists may scoff at this, at the debasement of coins, and at the many other financial dishonesties and enormities, as they are pleased to call them, of the Dark Ages; but let me tell them, who am also a bullionist, in so far that I recognize the superior economy, stability, and justice of a money system consisting of, or at least based representatively, wholly or in part, upon, the precious metals, that society could not have been preserved without these measures. Mankind had paid dearly enough in nine long centuries of tyranny, anarchy, and slavery for the

---

*Travels, 2, 173. †Marco Polo.

boon of a common medium of exchange. To have paid any more for it would have been to pay with life itself, for that, which, at the best, could only economize its labor and alleviate its burdens.

These fiscal measures not only eked out the scanty and stationary stock of coin which existed at that period; they economized its use, saved it from abrasion and loss, added to the rapidity of its circulation, made it perform double work, and thus bridged over the five hundred years of further dearth of money which was to continue until the discovery of America.

It is hardly worth while to specifically trace the wonderful and beneficial effects of the relief thus obtained or the era of industrial activity, commercial enterprise, and political enfranchisement to which it contributed, and which it is quite safe to say could not have occurred without it. The financial history of the past three hundred years is sufficiently familiar to every one, and all that is necessary in this place is to insert Mr. Jacob's hypothetical table of the increasing stock of the precious metals following the Dark Ages:

Year, A. D.	Stock of Coin.
1066	£34,600,000
1500	34,000,000
1546	49,400,000
1600	126,600,000

The ancient mode of obtaining the precious metals has been described. It consisted of washing auriferous sands and picking with rude instruments such scanty deposits of pure metal as could be found. With the invention of bronze tools and of smelting furnaces, a great impetus was afforded to mining, and this was increased by the invention of iron tools. It was in this condition that the art stood at the Roman era, the use of mercury in quickening and perfecting the process of recovering the precious metals not having been acquired until after the discovery of America. The 16th and 17th centuries therefore gave to the European world three great sources of increase to its stock of the precious metals: 1. The stock despoiled of the West India Islanders, the Mexicans and the Peruvians. 2. The new and great mines of Central America and Peru. 3d. The use of mercury in the amalgamation of ores.

Notwithstanding all these new and additional sources of supply, so utter had been the exhaustion of the European world's stock of gold and silver, so eager was the demand for these metals, so rapidly were they absorbed in the arts, in the Asiatic trade,* and by abrasion and loss, that the world's supply again came to a stand-still shortly after the beginning of the present century. The following are Mr. Jacob's hypothetical figures, which, for the period toward which we are now approaching, must be regarded as corroborated by the various careful computations of Humboldt and other authors. The reduction to dollars is at the rate of five to the pound sterling:

Year A. D.	Stock of coin in the commercial world.	Authority.
1700	$1,445,000,000	Jacob.
1700	1,318,000,000	Tooke.
1809	1,687,000,000	Gerboux.
1809	1,849,000,000	Tooke.
1827	1,720,000,000	Humboldt.
1829	1,557,000,000	Jacob.
1830	1,600,000,000	Storch.
1839	1,420,000,000	Storch.

The social phenomena of this period are too widespread and too directly traceable to monetary disturbances to admit of much doubt as to their connection with the decline in the world's stock of coin. To say nothing of the French revolution and the wars and great political events to which it gave rise—all of which, if they did not spring from, were certainly precipitated by, the unendurable poverty and suf-

*Humboldt's statement on this subject would lead to the inference that Asia had taken two-thirds of the entire American supply. Forbonnais supposes that between 1492 and 1724 Asia took one-half of the American supply, and Gerboux's estimate even exceeds this. Mr. Jacob, who reviewed them all, settled down to the opinion that Asia took two-fifths of the American supply between 1700 and 1810. (Jacob, p. 307.)

ferings of the French peasantry, which culminated in riots for bread and the distribution of wealth—this period is characterized by disorders all over Europe. The Newcastle and Scotch banks in Great Britain suspended in 1793, the Bank of St. Petersburgh suspended in 1796, the Bank of England in 1797, and again in 1822.* It was during this period that arose the State and provincial banking systems of this country and Great Britain, through which the actual and threatened dearth of money was alleviated by means of circulating notes representing but a small basis of specie. These desperate and unsafe expedients always evince a scarcity of the precious metals. It was during this period that these systems failed over and over again, not, however, without answering for precious intervals of time the important purpose of their establishment. The State banks of the United States failed in 1816, 1819, and 1827, and signally in 1837. The provincial banks of England in 1826 and 1847. Specie payments were suspended in France in 1790, and an enormous issue of assignats and mandats followed. As for the American suspension of 1837 it was felt all over the commercial world, which it shook to its foundations.

What had happened? Some people say wars; others, over-speculation. Perhaps they are right. Causation is a difficult science. But certainly the well attested decrease in the stock of the precious metals which occurred at about the beginning of the century may have had, and, in my opinion did have, much to do with these events. In fact, as Mr. Patterson has shown in his "Economy of Capital," they were in every case preceeded by an export and local scarcity of specie.

Be this as it may, two new sources of relief were hastening to the assistance of society. 1. The adaptation of steam to the processes of mining; 2. The discovery or rather rediscovery of the Ural mines, and the subsequent and more important opening of California and Australia. The new mines were discovered first. The adaptation of

---

*An abortive attempt to resume specie payments was made in 1817. (McLeod's Dict. Polit. Econ., I, 99.)

steam to their development came much later—indeed, belongs to the past few years.

The following are the statistics of the amount of specie added to the stock of the commercial world from 1848 to 1865:

Year A. D.	Stock of specie in the commercial world.	Authority.
1848–'53	$2,500,000,000	McCulloch.
1857–'60	2,800,000,000	Ruggles.
1872	3,600,000,000	Ernest Seyd.

The following are the estimates of various authorities of the stock of gold coin (only) in the commercial or Occidental world since 1848:

Year A. D.	Stock of gold coin in the commercial world.	Authority.
1848	$1,200,000,000	Chevalier.
1848	1,332,000,000	Est. on Newmarch.
1848	1,090,000,000	Est. on Levasseur.
1849	1,306,000,000	Jacob.
1853	1,464,000,000	Est. on Waguelin.
1860	1,998,000,000	Est. on Newmarch.
1860	2,209,000,000	Est. on Newmarch.
1867	2,600,000,000	Ruggles.
1872	2,600,000,000	Ernest Seyd.

With this vast and refreshing increment of specie, which more than filled the void left by the failure of the superficially-worked mines of Mexico and South America at the close of the last century, a new era of industrial activity, progress and development awaited society; an era which, if entered upon without reserve, might have crowded ten years into one, advanced us a century beyond the present time, and conferred upon each individual of to-day, the practical benefits of longevity.

But it was *not* entered upon without reserve. The plutocrats of Europe took alarm at the rapid increase of specie. They could manage to dispose of the surface-washings of gold in California and Australia, but they feared the application of steam machinery to the quartz veins of the Sierra

Nevadas, and they put their long heads together and conspired to cheat labor and enterprise of their reward and mankind of the main element of its circulating media. This was effected by the Demonetization of Silver.

To succinctly trace the narrative of this ingenious financial device carries us back to the point from which I diverged in order to sketch the history of the Supply and Consumption of the precious metals in Europe.

The course of the narrative will now be in respect of the relative value of gold and silver.

HISTORY OF THE RELATIVE VALUE OF GOLD AND SILVER.

This history naturally divides itself into four periods: The Ancient, Medieval, Modern, and Recent. The first extending from the most remote times to the beginning of the Christian era or failure of the ancient mines; the second extending from the last-named period when the effects of the discovery of Potosi were first felt; the third from that period to the year 1865, or the date of the arbitrary partial demonetization of silver by five nations; the fourth period to the present time. The accounts which have come down to us of the Ancient Period are inexact and partial. The relation is either stated in round figures by some careless author or calculated from laws the precise meaning and application of which are not beyond dispute. Each of these accounts relate to a single country, sometimes to a single city, and centuries occur between the date of one account and another. Such as they are, they are given herewith:

Table showing the Ratio of gold and silver in various countries of the World during the Ancient Period.

B. C.	*Ratio.*	*Authorities*
1600	13.33	Inscriptions at Karnak, tribute lists of Thutmosis. (Brandis.)
708	13.33	Cuneiform inscriptions on plates found in foundation of Khorsabad.
–	13.33	Ancient Persian coins; gold darics at 8.3 grams=20 silver siglos, at 5.5 grams.
500	13.00	Persia. Darius. Egyptian tribute. Herod. III, 95. (Bœckh, p. 12.)

Table—Continued.

B. C.	*Ratio.*	*Authorities.*
490	12.50	Sicily. Time of Gelon. "At least" 12.50. (Bœckh, p. 44.)
470	10.00	Doubtful. Asia Minor. Xerxes' treasure. (Bœckh, p. 11.)
440	13.00	Herodotus' account of Indian tributes. 360 gold talents=4,680 silver.
420	10.00	Asia Minor. Pay of Xenophon's troops in silver darics. (Anab.; Bœckh, p. 34.)
407	-	Spurious and debased gold coins at Athens. (McLeod, Polit. Econ., p. 476; Bœckh, p. 35.)
400	13.33	Standard in Asia, according to Xenophon.
400	12.00	Standard in Greece, according to "Hipparchus;" attributed to Plato.
400	12.00	Various authorities adduced by Bœckh.
400	13.50	
400	15.00	
404–336	12.00, 13.00, 13.33	Values in Greece from the Peloponnesian war to the time of Alexander, according to hints in Greek writers. There were variations under special contracts—unit, the silver drachma.
340	14.00	Greece. Time of Demosthenes. (Bœckh, p. 44.)
338–326	11.50	Special contracts in Greece.
343–323	12.50	Egypt under the Ptolemies.
300	10.00	Greece. Continued depression of gold, caused by great influx under Alexander.
207	13.70	Rome. (Bœckh, p. 44.) Gold scriptulum arbitrarily fixed at 17.143 for 1.
100	11.91	Rome. General rate of gold pound to silver sesterces to date.
58–49	8.93	Rome. Continued depression of gold, caused by influx of Cæsar's spoil from Gaul. [N. B.—Cæsar's head-quarters were at Aquileia, at the head of the Adriatic, where there was also a gold mine, which at this period became very prolific.]
50	11.90	Rome. "About the year U. C. 700" the rate was $11\frac{1}{2}\frac{9}{1}$. (Bœckh, p. 44.)
29	12.00	Rome. Normal rate in the last days of the republic.
A. D.		
1–37	11.97	Rome. Rate under Augustus and Tiberius.

None but the gravest events—events which affected many nations, and were felt through long periods of time, sufficed to disturb this relation. The two most noteworthy of these were the vast spoil of Alexander, which he gathered in the Orient and brought into Europe, and the spoil of Cæsar in Gaul, which he sent to Rome by way of Aquileia. These events temporarily depressed gold from the ratio of 12 to that of 10, in the first instance, and from 12 to 8, in the second; but the depression was both local and temporary. Omitting these temporary aberrations, the general range of the ratio in Ancient times, so far as the evidence now available furnishes ground for opinion, seems to have been about from 12 to 13.33.

The accounts relating to the Medieval Period partake more or less of the characteristics peculiar to the ancient. Lesser intervals of time intervene between the dates, lesser distances between the countries, and lesser differences between the rates in one country compared with another. Nevertheless, the condition of medieval society was too unconnected, and the arbitrary and conflicting laws governing the production, consumption, and legal attributes of the precious metals in various countries, are too little understood at the present day, if, indeed, they ever were fully understood, to render these quotations of practical value. They will be found below:

Table showing the Ratio of gold and silver in various countries of the World during the Medieval Period. Range 11.44 @ 13.51.

A. D.	*Ratio.*	*Authorities.*	
37–41	12.17	Rome. Reign of Caligula.	The silver coinage much debased, consequently the ratio of the metals, pure, was as about 1 to 11.
54–68	11.80	Rome. Reign of Nero.	
69–79	11.54	Rome. Reign of Vespasian.	
81–96	11.30	Rome. Reign of Domitian.	
138–161	11.98	Rome. Reign of Antoninus.	
312	14.40	Byzantium. Reign of Constantine. Arbitrary.	
438	14.40	Byzantium and Rome. Theodosian Code. Arbitrary.	
864	12.00	Probable ratio, as shown by the *Edictum Pistense*, under the Carlovingian dynasty.	
1260	10.50	Average ratio in the commercial cities of Italy. Local or doubtful.	
1344–1660	——	England. Numerous mint indentures given in McLeod's Political Economy, p. 475. The ratio, except when fixed arbitrarily and in violation of market price, varied between about 1:12 and 1:14 during the two hundred and fifty-seven years included in this period.	
1351	12.30	Ratio in North Germany as shown by the very accurate rules of the Lubeck mint, corroborated in the main by the accounts of the Teutonic Order of Knights, averaged in periods of forty years.	
1375	12.40		
1403	12.80		
1411	12.00		
1451	11.70		
1463	11.60		
1455–1494	10.50	Ratio according to the accounts of the Teutonic Knights. As the ratio fixed in England by numerous mint indentures from 1465 to 1509 was about 1:12, this German ratio is considered local or doubtful.	
1497	10.70	Spain. Reign of Isabella. Edict of Medina. Local.	
1500	10.50	Germany. Adam Riese's Arithmetic. Local or doubtful.	

Table—Continued.

A. D.	*Ratio.*	*Authorities.*
1551	11.17	Germany. Imperial Mint regulations. Arbitrary or local.
1559	11.44	German Imperial Mint regulations.
1561	11.70	France. Mint regulations.
1575	11.68	France. Mint regulations.
1623	11.74	Upper Germany. Mint regulations.
1640	13.51	France. Mint regulations. Transition period.

The extreme range of all of the above quotations which are considered even measuredly reliable is from 11.44 to 13.51, the latter a single instance at the close of the period and after the opening of the American mines. Most of the quotations come within the range of from 11.70 to 12.40, which, considering that the table covers a period of sixteen centuries and numerous countries but little connected by commerce until a late period, serves to show the remarkable constancy of the relation between the metals.

From the time of the conquest of England, A. D. 1066, until the reign of Edward III there was no gold coined in England,* and probably none in circulation, and this was doubtless substantially the case also in Continental Europe. Taking this inference in connection with the commonness and large size of gold coins in ancient times, we are justified in ascribing the decrement of coin during the medieval ages rather to the falling off in the supplies of gold than to that of silver and the fluctuation of the ratio, such as it was, to the aberrations of the gold supply.

We have thus an additional corroboration of the superior stability of silver to gold: a corroboration still further strengthened by the fact that silver alone was, in fact, if not always legally, the standard in England † and throughout Europe up to about the beginning of the present century.

For the Modern Period we have more reliable data. This results from the fact that during this period countries be-

---

* Essay on coins by Martin Folkes, London, about 1750, quoted in Harris on Coins, ii, 2.

† Harris, i, 61; ii, 85 and ii, 106–7.

came united by commerce; and quotations in one hold good with slight variation for all the others. As at about the commencement of this period all those events occurred which have had any material influence in altering between the metals the relation which previously existed, to wit, the opening of the East India and China trade, the opening of the American mines, and the use of quicksilver in the amalgamation of ores, it is wholly useless in this or any other practical connection, to consult any other data concerning the relation of the metals with the view of determining such relation for the future.

Table showing the Ratio of gold and silver in various countries of the World during the Modern Period, or since the opening of the East India and China trade. Range 14.74 @ 15.83.

A. D.	*Ratio.*	*Country.*	*Authorities.*
1665	15.10	France.	Mint regulations.
1667	14.15	Upper Germany.	Mint regulations. Doubtful.
1669	15.11	Upper Germany.	Mint regulations.
1670–1817	——	England.	Numerous mint regulations quoted by McLeod.
1679	15.00	France.	Mint regulations.
1680	15.40	France.	Mint regulations.
1687–1700	14.97	Hamburg.	Ratios calculated from the bi-weekly quotations of the Hamburg prices-current, giving the value of the gold ducats of Holland in silver thalers down to 1771, and after that in fine silver bars. The nominal par of exchange during this period was 1:14.80, and the quotations show the variations of the market rate in percentage above or below this. At par, 6 silver marks-banco were equivalent to 1 ducat; 68 20-47 ducats containing 1 mark (weight) of fine gold, and $27\frac{3}{4}$ silver marks-banco containing 1 mark (weight) of fine silver. Hence, 6×68 20-47÷$27\frac{3}{4}$= 14.80, the par ratio.
1701–1720	15.21		
1721–1740	15.08		
1741–1790	14.74		
1791–1800	15.42		
1801–1810	15.61		
1811–1820	15.51		
1821–1830	15.80		
1831–1840	15.67		
1841–1850	15.83		
1851	15.46	England.	London market quotations—annual averages. These give the price of a given weight of standard silver in shillings and pence. The standard gold is $\frac{11}{12}$ths fine, and an ounce Troy is coined into 934.5 pence, or an ounce of fine
1852	15.57		
1853	15.33		
1854	15.33		
1855	15.36		
1856	15.33		
1857	15.27		
1858	15.36		
1859	15.21		
1860	15.30		

Table—Continued.

A. D.	*Ratio.*	*Country.*	*Authorities.*
1861	15.47	England.	gold into 1019.45 pence. The standard silver is $\frac{37}{40}$ths fine. Hence, as fine silver is worth 1.081 times as much as standard silver, if 1019.45 pence be divided by 1.081 times the quoted price of an ounce of standard silver, the quotient is the ratio desired.
1862	15.36		
1863	15.38		
1864	15.40		
1865	15.33		
1866	15.44		
1867	15.57		
1868	15.60		
1869	15.60		
1870	15.60		
1871	15.59		
1872	15.63		

A glance at this table shows that the extreme range of fluctuation for a period of over two hundred years, closing with the year 1872, was 14.74 to 15.83. Most of the quotations are close to 15½ of silver to 1 of gold. The change from the relation which existed during the medieval period is attributable chiefly to the opening of the Oriental trade by the way of the Cape of Good Hope, and the settlement of the different relations between gold and silver which existed in the Oriental and Occidental worlds. This settlement took place during the seventeenth century; since which time the ratio has remained almost stationary and uniform throughout the world.

I have already stated that the East India trade absorbed a large proportion, estimated at two-fifths, of the whole American product of the precious metals; that is to say, about one-fifth during the seventeenth century and one-fifth during the eighteenth. This proportion consisted nearly altogether of silver. The result of these shipments of silver to the Orient was, that of the supplies of American metal absorbed in Europe, a large portion consisted of gold. With the rise in prices which followed the discovery of America the demand for supplies of gold, as against silver, in Europe, was greater than before, owing to the superior availability of gold at that period for large payments; a superiority which the subsequent growth of banks and places of deposit has now destroyed. This slightly increased demand for gold as against silver must be set off against the urgent demand for silver in the Orient.

The average ratio at Hamburgh for the twenty years, 1701–1720, is given in the table at 15.21. Sir Isaac Newton, in his report on coins, dated 1717, estimated it at 14.8 to 15 throughout Europe.

At this period the legal relation in England was 15½ and silver was, therefore, undervalued by law. The consequence was that a large portion of the silver coin was exported to countries where it was more justly estimated. To remedy the loss of coinage involved in exportation, the weight of the gold pieces was lessened, and instead of 890, there were coined out of a pound of standard gold 934½ sovereigns of 20 shillings, or their equivalent, 890, in guineas of 21 shillings; or, what is the same thing, the guinea, or pound of guinea gold, of 20 shillings, was ordered to pass current at 21 shillings.

We are told by modern apologists for the adoption of the single gold standard in England in 1816, without any support for such statement, that the single gold standard was practically the standard of England from the time of this change in the coinage by Sir Isaac Newton.* But this fact, however "practical," had nothing whatever to do with the law on the subject.

It appears that some forty years after Newton's coinage reform, gold fell in the markets of Europe until it would only purchase 14.74 of silver, while the law valued it at slightly under.† Such being the case, there arose an agitation favorable to the payment in gold of the interest or principal on the public debt, which was then largely held abroad.‡ The argument in favor of this project was entirely sound. The debt had been incurred in "pounds." The "pound" was a money of account consisting of 20 actual shillings of silver, each 11 ounces 2 dwts. fine, out of 12 ounces, and weighing 3 ounces 17 dwts. 10 grains; in other words, one pound Troy weight, of standard silver,

---

* McLeod.

†2 Harris, p. 54, appears to make it 14.145, but this is unprecise.

‡2 Harris, 53–106.

was coined into 62 of these shillings. By the same mint indenture a pound Troy of standard gold was coined into as many guineas as there were in 890 shillings, and by subsequent indentures, previous to the period of the dispute, into as many sovereigns as there were in 934½ shillings.* Why not, then, pay the debt in these gold "guineas?"

The only doubt which could arise as to the equity of this proceeding depended upon the fact as to when (under what indentures) the debt had been incurred, though, in fact, this question was of no importance. But it never seemed to have troubled the disputants, who represented that large and influential portion of the debt which was held at home. They stood upon the pound of silver; declared that that was the sole standard of value; that gold coins were mere tokens, and that the honor of the Crown was involved in the payment of the debt in silver "pounds," which, in point of fact, was only a money of account,† and had had no actual existence in silver since the days of William of Normandy, and none at all in gold.

The superior talent or persistency of these advocates of plutocracy prevailed over reason and equity, as it prevailed afterwards, when they took the opposite side of the argument and showed that gold was the standard of England, and not silver; as it has prevailed in this Chamber; as it has prevailed everywhere and at all times. The books and pamplets issued on the subject at this period were innumerable, and amidst the confusion which they occasioned, the unaccustomed jargon of the mint, and the loud voices of the plutocratical orators, the latter carried the day, and silver was assented to be the sole standard of England.

Some seventy years later, while specie payments were suspended in England, and there was no currency in circulation except unrepresentative and irredeemable bank notes, silver was demonetized by law, as McLeod says it

*McLeod, Appendix, pp. 9, 10.

†1 Harris, i., 61; Ibid., ii, pp. 85, 97.

had been in fact since the period of the measures effected by Sir Isaac Newton,* and, except for payments up to 40 shillings, gold was declared the sole standard of value.

This celebrated Enactment, the first one specifically making gold the single standard of value which was adopted by any country, is attributed to the same sinister influence which unhistorically and illogically maintained in 1750–57, that silver was or ought to be the sole standard of England, because at that period gold had become slightly the cheaper metal of the two, at the relation denoted by the mint indentures, which had existed in Isaac Newton's time. But this inference does not appear to be supported either by the market ratio of the metals at that time, or by any other facts known to the authors or supporters of the enactment. The chief of these supporters was Lord Liverpool, whose report on coins antedates by several years the great work of Humboldt on New Spain, and by many years that of Jacob on the History of the Precious Metals. The principal fact in this connection which was known at that time, and which could have influenced the adoption of the single gold standard, was that silver had been slowly falling in value since the period of the bank suspension. The average market ratio for the decade ending in 1790, was 14.74; while for the decade ending in 1800, it was 15.42, and for that ending in 1810, it was 15.61. Beyond this, the supporters of the act of 1816 knew little or nothing which could have assisted them in forming a judgment with regard to the probable future course of the metals. The act of 1816 was therefore a mere blunder, a piece of empiricism based at most upon a recent, and as it afterwards proved, a mere trifling and temporary, decline of silver. When we come to trace its consequences we shall see what a deplorable blunder it

---

*The authorities on this subject, viz: Harris, 1757, Chevallier, 1857, McLeod, Patterson, and Seyd, disagree as to the legal position of the standard of England from 1717 to 1816. The truth appears to be that the standard was the double one.

was. And it is just such a blunder that we would now commit in this country if we disregard the present opportunity of restoring the double standard, if we empirically refuse to recognize silver as an essential and component part of the money of the world, simply because, for the moment, the ratio of silver to gold is depressed.

Having now traced the standard of England down to its latest legal change, which occurred in 1816, it need only be stated briefly in this place that no other country adopted the gold standard, except Portugal, until 1865. The standards of the various principal countries of the Occidental world previous to 1865 were either of silver, as in Germany, Holland, Scandinavia, etc., or of gold and silver equally, as in France, Spain, the United States, Belgium, &c. During the interval between 1809 and 1848, when gold was falling off in supply and rising in price, England entered upon that policy of lending in silver and demanding payment in gold, which, but for the widespread bankruptcies which the failure of the gold supplies contributed to occasion in 1837, would have greatly enriched her wealthy classes. They lent capital to all the countries of the world, lent in the cheaper moneys of those countries, (as they lent us later still during our civil war in paper,) and always demanded payment in gold. Like all short-sighted policies, it was a profitable thing, so long as it lasted, but its very profitableness forbade it to last.

The creditor may seek support in unjust laws, but nature is on the side of the debtor, and nature redresses the inequalities of laws. As to the effect upon her own people in demonetizing silver during the period when gold was rising in value, it need only be said, that England never passed through a more gloomy period than during the half century preceding the opening of California. One has only to read Professor Thorold Rogers's Review of Agriculture and Prices in England from the thirteenth to the nineteenth centuries, and McKay's Working Classes, to be convinced of the fact that during the period, 1816–48, the English laborer was reduced to a condition but little better than that of his predecessors during the Middle Ages, and infinitely worse than that of his predecessors a century before.

Money became scarce, and despite the alleviation caused by the invention of banking and paper money, hard times set in. After 1809 the annual supply of the precious metals declined fully one-half, owing to the stoppage of the Mexican mines, consequent upon the war between Spain and her American colonies. The period when the precious metals were most scarce was between 1810 and 1840; and this, as every one knows, was precisely the period when national distress and political agitation were most rife among us. The masses suffered and clamored for Reform; the middle classes groaned under the taxation and cried for Retrenchment; and in Parliament there arose the policy of Peace, to lessen the burdens of a nation which could not afford to go to war. The discovery of the Ural mines of Russia thereafter began to mitigate, though not to remove the dearth. But now, once more a change has taken place, and the discovery of the rich mines of California, Columbia, and Australia, &c. (Patterson's Econ. of Capital, p. 45.)

There is another point in this connection which is well worth mentioning to those who have shown so much eagerness to lead this country into the unwise footsteps which England has trodden in respect of the standard of money. It may, perhaps, not have occurred to them that with a system of household suffrage, such as exists in England, the slightest rise in values has the effect of extending the franchise of voting. This was shown by Mr. Patterson in his Economy of Capital, pp. 60, *et seq:*

"Houses which rented at £8 in 1848 are now rented at £10, which secures the franchise for the occupiers. * * Taking the case of England in the nineteen years before the new gold supplies came into play we find that between 1832 and 1851, the registered electors for burghs increased one-half and those for counties more than one-third, while the total population increased less than one-third."

Here, then, is a reason, in addition to their pecuniary interest, which actuates the ruling classes of England in their monetary legislation, a reason that should teach us of America to beware what hidden pits we may fall into by blindly and subserviently following the politico-economical or legislative footsteps, be they backward or forward, of a foreign country.

We need no foreign advice in the great concerns of State. When that greatest of all political events—the American Revolution, which not only gave freedom to this people, but for the first time in the history of the world divorced Church and State, denied the "divine right" of kings, the privileges of class, and the claims of feudalism, and thus gave to all men at once the principles of government and a land in which those principles could be carried into practice—when the American Revolution was organized, did our forefathers send to ask the opinion of the ruling classes of Europe? No. They knew that if they did so the answer that they would get would be unfavorable to the accomplishment of their ends. These ends were the freedom and happiness of all men. These are what they had fought for and determined upon, and they needed no advice as to how they should secure them in that organization of a State which had been committed to their charge.

We now come to the effects of the gold discoveries in California, which effects, preceded as those discoveries had been, by the minor ones of Ural and Siberia, were felt soon after the events that gave rise to them. At this period, about the year 1850, England still had the single gold standard, the United States the double standard at 16, France the double standard at 15½; Spain, Holland and Belgium,* the double standard; and Germany, Naples,† and other countries, the single silver standard. In a word, the silver unit (dollar, thaler, franc, real, or rouble) was a legal tender to an unlimited extent in all these countries except England.

---

*Chevalier, pp. 6, 157, 159, 163. †Ibid., p. 169.

When gold began to pour in from the shores of the Pacific the first and very proper act of the United States and France was to coin gold pieces and use them instead of silver ones for legal tender. The United States, still holding on to her double standard, stopped coining the silver dollar, and by the act of 1853, coined a gold one, because it was the cheaper one. France also held on to her double standard (of 15½) notwithstanding the eloquence of Chevalier, who, like Harris in England, precisely a century before, tried to convince France that the law of 7th Germenal, Anno XI, (year 1803,) meant a single silver standard instead of a double one. The first care of these two great republics was the interests of their people, and these interests they consulted when they held on to a system which looks to and utilizes the whole supply of the precious metals for the basis of commercial transactions.

Holland and Belgium pursued a different course. These countries, like England, were governed by kings, surrounded by a powerful plutocracy. Like her they were lenders of money, the creditors of other nations, and like her they feared the fall of gold. But unlike England, they had had no single gold standard before; no gold standard while gold was becoming scarce, as during the period 1816–1840; therefore no distress, no agitations, no Chartist riots, no reform bills, no clamor for popular representation, no demand for ministerial responsibility. Hence, unlike the British plutocrats, those of Holland and Belgium had no fears to restrain them from adopting a single silver standard when silver became dear. Belgium retired her gold coins in 1854,* and adopted a silver standard. Holland did the same thing in 1858.†

---

* After having cut off her own tail, Belgium, through the agency of her distinguished plutocratical politico-economist M. Gustave de Molinari, endeavored to induce France to do the same thing. This effort was made through the medium of the pages of the *Economiste Belge* of 10th February, 1857, in which M. Molinari recommended France to demonetize gold by reducing her gold coins to tokens, and adopt the single silver standard after Belgium.

† McCulloch Dic., Art. "Precious Metals," says 1847 and 1849.

The success of the ruling classes in Holland and Belgium in demonetizing gold during this period of its downfall was greatly envied by their brethren in England. Between 1850 and 1857 gold fell from 15.83 to 15.27 of silver, the extremest range, as it has since proved, during more than eighty years, to wit, from 1790 to 1872. The creditor classes of England viewed this depression of their favored metal with great alarm, and fancied that it would go on—as with the same short-sightedness they now fancy that the present temporary depression of silver will go on—forever. Forgetting that they had profited while gold rose, they now demanded that they should not lose because gold was falling. They looked with envy upon the plutocratical legislation of Holland and Belgium, and asked why England should not also demonetize gold and adopt silver as her sole standard of value.

Unfortunately for them, their own short-sighted and blundering legislation of 1816 stood in the way, and Nature was reaping its revenge. What was to be done? What had England's plutocratical politico-economists to advise at this period?

Mr. Richard Cobden, while disclaiming any right on the part of the government to interfere with contracts already made, saw no reason why it should be excluded from such interference with the future as might be necessary to facilitate voluntary contracts. (Chevalier, p. 6.)

Mr. James Maclaren recommended the establishment of life insurance companies on the basis of a silver standard. (Ibid.)

Mr. Cobden, quoting this suggestion with approbation, proposed to adapt it to all contracts extending over a long period of time, and even thought of evading the consequences of the depreciation of gold by resorting to the primitive practice of paying in kind, as by granting farm leases upon a rent to be regulated by the price of produce!* O sophistry, sophistry, how desperate are thy convolutions!

---

*In Jevon's latest work Messrs. Scrope & Lewis are quoted as in favor of adopting the average of one hundred articles of produce as the measure of value.

In short, England was fairly caught in her own toils, and, but for the retention of the double standard in the United States, France, and other countries, which enabled these countries to absorb the new supplies of gold by replacing with them their silver coins, which they exported to Asia, wherewith to pay for goods, the relations of commodities and services in England—and this involved her entire political structure—would have been revolutionized. As it was, her government barely escaped overthrow, and the agency that saved her was that very double standard which the selfishness and folly of 1816 had overthrown in England, but which, fortunately for England, other nations had retained.

The consequences of these various measures, during the fall of gold from 1848 to 1865, were that England prospered in spite of her foiled plutocracy, France prospered, and the United States prospered, and an era of industrial activity was opened in these three great countries the like of which had never been seen before. This was the distinctive era of labor-saving machines, international expositions, railways, life insurance, clearing-houses, and great commercial reforms.

THE RECENT PERIOD.

Table showing the ratio of gold and silver, chiefly in the London market, during the Recent Period, or since the Demonetization of Silver effected by the act of February* 12, 1873. *Range* 15.9 @ 17.82.

Year.	Ratio.	Country.		Authorities.
1873----	15.90	England.	Annual av'g calculated as above.	
1874----	16.15	England.	" " " "	
1875----	16.45	England.	January ---	Average 16.45
1875----	16.41	England.	February--	
1875----	16.50	England.	March -----	
1875----	16.47	England.	April ------	Average 16.63
1875----	16.55	England.	May -------	
1875----	16.88	England.	June -------	

*The table from which the quotations for 1875 and 1876 are obtained is "deduced from quotations on the London and New York markets."

Table—Continued.

Year.	Ratio.	Country.		Authorities.
1875----	16.97	England.	July.	Average 16.88
1875----	16.92	England.	August.	
1875----	16.74	England.	September.	
1875----	16.74	England.	October ---	Average 16.79
1875----	16.75	England.	November-	
1875----	16.89	England.	December-	
1876----	17.08	England.	January ---	Average 17.45
1876----	17.46	England.	February--	
1876----	17.82	England.	March -----	
1876----	17.69	England.	To April 12.	--------- 17.69

We now come to the next important change in the history of money and the standard—the era of the silver-bearing mines of the Comstock lode, of the demonetization of silver in several important countries of continental Europe, and its demonetization in the United States through the agency of the act of 1873.

This era opened in 1862 with the exportation of the entire stock of silver, as well as other coin, of the United States, consequent upon the adoption of an unrepresentative paper currency by the act of February 25th of that year. In the same year also occurred the discovery of the great silver-bearing mines of Washoe.

The ratio of silver to gold in the markets of the world was thus threatened with depression from two causes acting simultaneously: 1. The demonetization of a large stock of coin by an important country; 2. The discovery of new and very productive silver mines. It was not forgotten by financiers that, together with our silver, we demonetized a much more valuable stock of gold, nor that Washoe was still in its incipiency. Therefore, it was not until 1863 or 1864 that the bearing of the events of 1862 upon the probable future ratio of silver and gold began to be discussed in Europe. Their bearing, however, was not wholly dismissed from consideration, and as the Washoe mines gave more and more promise of great production, discussion in Europe with regard to the tendency of the ratio became more and more common.

In England the anticipated decline of silver was regadred with great complacency. It was a veritable windfall for her plutocracy; a parachute to retard the previously threatening decline in the purchasing power of gold; a governor to that engine of their own construction, which they had built in 1816 and regretted since 1848.

As the great mines of Washoe became further developed the continental plutocracy also began to prick up its ears. It was at this period organized and formidable, which is more than can be said of it in 1848, when the Red flag flaunted in its face from every corner of Europe. France was now an empire; Italy a united kingdom; Greece a newly fledged monarchy. The plutocrats of these countries could have their own way now.

Nature, steam, and the Comstock lode labored for mankind; the silver treasures of the Sierra Nevada began to make themselves felt in the coinages; the gold product fell off, and gold went up to nearly 16 of silver. It was therefore in the interests of the plutocracies to demonetize silver and adopt gold as the sole standard of value, and they endeavored to convince society that gold alone was the true standard.

The reading world was flooded with pamphlets and magazine articles on the subject, penned by the highest order of talent, which, too often neglected by the people, is forced to ally itself with power; conventions, with cut-and-dried programmes, were called to discuss the matter; advocates were employed and charlatans retained to drown with the clamor of numbers the modest voices of science, equity, and reason. Another motive urged the plutocracies to their course. So long as silver was harbored as a legal tender in Europe, the United States, by being the principal producer of that metal, might become the money center of the world—a matter of no little concern to London, Paris, and Berlin.

An international monetary convention was held in Paris in 1865, and a treaty concluded between France, Belgium, Italy, and Switzerland, in which Greece and Roumania subsequently joined, by virtue of which these countries so limited the mintage of their legal tender silver coins as to prepare to make gold their sole standard of value, and partially demonetize silver. Taught by previous experience, they did not actually demonetize silver, but left the law in such a condition that by a concerted change in the coinage regulations, either gold or silver, if need be, could be made the sole legal tender, and by adopting whatever happened to be for the time, the dearer metal, a see-saw between silver and gold could be kept up for the benefit of plutocracy at every change of market relation.

There can be no see-saw unless the legal relation between the metals is permanently fixed and unalterable. When this relation is altered from time to time, as it should be, (once in ten or twenty years would practically be often enough,) to accord with the slow fluctuations of the markets, neither the creditor who would demand the dearer metal, nor the debtor who would proffer the cheaper metal, could profit by having his choice. But when the relation is unalterably fixed or difficult to alter, as is the case in France, then the creditor who receives in the metal that abroad commands a premium, or the debtor who pays in the one that can be purchased abroad at a discount in the one which is the legal tender, derives an advantage. It is the monkey and the cheese between the two cats.

This treaty of 1865 was to last until 1880, and with certain modifications is still in force. England did not enter into it. Gold was now to become dearer, and in her present political condition, when popular interests have the power to be heard, her plutocrats feared to open a question which might overthrow the advantages they already possessed. England had a single and peremptory gold standard. Why should she enter into a treaty which would make her a party to only a permissive gold standard, a standard which, practically, when the treaty expired, and before gold fell in price again, might be changed by a concerted coinage regulation?

But although British plutocracy saw nothing to be gained

by entering into the monetary treaty of 1865, it saw something to be gained by attending the Congress which preceded the treaty and the subsequent convention which was held in 1867 with the view to extend the operation of the treaty. That something was to draw the United States into the treaty, the United States which were, as yet, not bound to a gold standard at all, either permissive or obligatory.

Accordingly England sent her delegates to both conventions. They were instructed to say nothing which would bind England, but to carefully watch and report the proceedings until, I presume, the hands of the United States were fairly into the fire and the chestnuts safely landed for the benefit of the ruling classes of England. These instructions were carried out with great skill. The Frenchmen arranged the programme, the Germans did the arguing and philosophizing, the Englishmen listened, and the American delegate, overcome by the plutocratical atmosphere that surrounded him, walked straight into the trap that had been set for him. The convention was called for the nominal purpose of unitizing the weights of the coins of various nations. Its real object, which it fully accomplished, was to commit the United States to the adoption of the gold standard while gold was growing dearer, so that the interest and principal of her public, corporate, and mercantile indebtedness, held mainly in Europe, which was then under our laws payable in the silver dollar of 371¼ grains pure, should be made payable in the temporarily more valuable gold dollar of 23.22 grains pure. Of course the United States was not bound by this vote of its delegate in the International Monetary Convention, but the vote had its influence. It tended to sway the judgment of the Congress of the United States when the question came up, that is to say, tended to sway it so far as it was called into exercise at all.

DEBATE ON THE AMERICAN DEMONETIZATION ACT OF 1873.

But the manner in which this legislation was effected

leaves but little reason to infer that any deliberate judgment was exercised on this important subject of the standard, or that the question was ever so presented to the American people as to elicit the indorsement or the approval of any single congressional constituency. The bill by which it was effected, originated, as I understand it, in another bill which was introduced into the House of Representatives, February 9, 1872. It was discussed for a few moments on April 9, 1872. Then the discussion was cut short, and a substitute, the present law, reported by title on May 27, and passed without a reading, under a suspension of the rules, May 29, 1872. From the House it went to the Senate, where, without any discussion at all upon the all-important section fourteen, it passed; and, after concurrence by the House, again without a discussion, became a law.

I am aware that it has been stated that the bill was passed after very full discussion on this subject: but I am unable to find a corroboration of this statement in the official report of the proceedings. If any such full discussion appears in the *Record*, I shall be glad to have it pointed out, in order that I may correct the impression now on my mind in respect of this matter.

This bill was originally reported to the House of Representatives February 9, 1872, from the Committee on Coinage, Weights, and Measures, by its chairman, Mr. Hooper, of Massachusetts. It was discussed for the first time April 9, 1872, when Mr. Hooper informed the House that Mr. Ernest Seyd, of London, a distinguished writer on coins, had examined the first draft of the bill and "furnished many valuable suggestions which have been incorporated in the bill." Curiously enough, Mr. Seyd is an uncompromising advocate of the double standard, and it is to be regretted that having received Mr. Seyd's advice, the committee only saw fit to follow it wherein it was entirely unessential and to disregard it in its most important feature. Mr. Hooper then assured the House with regard to section fourteen, where the standard was changed by implication from the double to a single gold one, that the reason for this change was that the silver dollar was worth $1.03, a mere accidental and temporary fact which afforded no sound reason for abandoning the double standard. Subsequent events have proved that the option which we then enjoyed of paying in silver or gold dollars at pleasure was of the highest importance to the American people, and should not have been surrendered. Even if the fact as to the premium on the silver dollar were permanent and assured, the simple remedy would have been to change the legal relation between gold and silver.

Mr. Hooper also stated that the single gold standard had been adopted in Great Britain and most of the European countries, which latter statement was certainly not correct. (Cong. Record, 2d Sess., 42d Cong., part 3, p. 2305.)

Mr. Stoughton, who followed Mr. Hooper, repeated the statement that the silver dollar was worth, he said, 3¼ per cent. premium. (P. 2309.)

Mr. Kelley, who followed Mr. Stoughton, said it was worth 3½ per cent.. (Pp. 2311 and 2316.)

Mr. Potter, of New York, appeared to be the only member, beside the movers, who suspected the real character of the bill. He said, (p. 2310:) "I confess that the introduction of the bill at such a period (during a suspension of specie payments) excited my suspicion. I was and am at a loss to gather from anything I know or can learn that there is any necessity for the adoption of this measure now." Among the objections he had to the bill was that "it provides for the making of changes in the legal tender coin of the country, and for substituting as legal tender, coin of only one metal, instead as heretofore of two." (P. 2310.) Finally he stigmatized the bill as a cover, and that it was "gotten up to be a cover," among other things, for the coinage of nickel pieces in order to enhance the market value of nickel and benefit the monopolizers of nickel mines and processes. (P. 2312.)

And the impartial observer at the present time finds it

difficult to account for the introduction of such a bill when specie payments were suspended and unprovided for, unless upon some such ground as Mr. Potter suggested, to wit, either the interest of the owners of nickel mines at home or that of creditors at home or abroad.

But of what avail was argument or objection? The discussion was cut short by a motion to adjourn, and the discussion was never renewed. The next we hear of the bill is that it was pushed through on the 27th May, under a suspension of the rules, without even a reading, and that it went to the Senate. (P. 3883.) There it was reported by title on the 28th May, referred by title to the Finance Committee on the 29th May, and passed at the following session, without, so far as can be ascertained from the Congressional Record, having ever been fully considered.

CAUSES OF THE RELATION OF 15½.

Turning away from these details to the general history of the relative value of the precious metals, the principal and by far the most important fact to be observed is the remarkable steadiness which this relation has shown for over two hundred years.

The question now arises concerning this constancy in the relation in value of gold and silver since the early part of the seventeenth century. To what is it due? We have seen that this relation has been almost constantly, and with slight variation, 15½. Why has the pivotal point of this relation been just 15½? Why not 13, as in the days of Herodotus? Why not 12, as in the Feudal Ages? Why did it not fall to 20 when Potosi poured its silver treasures upon the world? In short, why did it center at 15½ and remain there? A satisfactory answer to this question cannot fail to be important, because it will afford a guide which will enable us to compute the probable variation of the relation between silver and gold in the future.

Since the opening of the East Indies and China trade in the early part of the seventeenth century the relation of gold and silver in the Occident and gold and silver in the Orient became equalized. At the same era, also, the Spanish-American silver mines were opened, and the use of quicksilver in amalgamating ores discovered. These three events changed the pre-existing relations in the whole world. The first raised the value of silver, the second and third lowered it; the three together placed it at 15½, kept it there, and equalized it all over the world. The Oriental trade continues, the American silver mines are still productive, the process of amalgamation is still employed. Therefore the conditions of production and consumption are essentially the same as they have been for over two hundred years. When we consult those conditions with the view of determining the cause of the relation between gold and silver, we find that the same quantity of capital, superintendence, labor, or of those commodities necessary to support capitalists, superintendents, and laborers, as food, clothing, shelter, &c., and of materials, such as quicksilver, tools, machines, &c., as are, on the average, employed to extract fifteen-and-a-half pounds of silver from the earth, will only produce one pound of gold. This is the average of all countries and of over two hundred years of trial. It comes to this at last. This is the boiling down of the whole subject.

It will, of course, be understood that the several rewards of capitalists, superintendents, and laborers, in other words, their share of production, differs in various countries, and has differed at various periods ever since the opening of India and America. So, also, has the effectiveness of laborers. Hence, the reward of each of these classes of persons has differed enormously. But, as under the same difficulties of production—and these have not changed as between the metals during the past two centuries, and are not likely to change in the future—the sum total of their contributions to the work has been the same, it follows that, as before stated, it is the total outlay of capital and labor, applied respectively to gold and silver, that has determined the relation of value between them.

When, at any given time or in any given country, the same outlay of capital, labor, materials, etc., that is sufficient to result in the production of one pound of gold, if removed from gold and applied to silver mining, will produce more than 15½ pounds of silver, the labor, materials, etc., will be removed from the production of gold to that of silver. When, at another time or in another place, the outlay sufficient to result in the production of 15½ pounds of silver if devoted, instead, to gold, will produce a fraction more than one pound of gold, it will, as a matter of course, be devoted to gold. The same laborers and the same capital, plant, tools, materials, etc., are not always removed from one industry to the other. One industry ceases in one place; the other may spring up in another place. It amounts to the same thing either way. These changes do not occur on the instant; they come about in time. When mines cease to be profitable at the long-established relation in value of silver and gold—a relation that finds its reflection in the prices of the services and commodities necessary to carry on the works—they are not abandoned at once, but continued in the hope of improvement. If no such improvement occurs they must eventually stop, for men will not and cannot go on forever losing money at mining.

This, then, is the basic reason for the long time relation in value of silver and gold. The average result of over two hundred years of experiment in all parts of the world assures us that 15½ pounds of silver and 1 pound of gold are equivalents, and this assurance is as solidly supported in respect of the future as we find it in respect of the past. Now that the most remote parts of the world are connected by commerce, nothing can weaken it, unless it were possible that some very great and peculiar improvement in mining or the recovery of ores could take place in respect of one metal and not of the other. For example, suppose an improved method of extracting or recovering gold was devised which was inapplicable to silver: then gold would be produced more cheaply than now and silver would rise in value, or *vice versa*, in case the improvement could be applied to silver and not to gold.

But this is impossible: first, because the nature and qualities of the two metals are so nearly alike that any improvement applicable to the extraction or recovery of one must apply also to the other; and, second, because the geological distribution of the two metals is such that, in many of the large deposits of the world, they lie together in the same matrix. They must therefore be taken out together, and the quartz which contains them both, must be crushed, amalgamated, separated, and refined by one and the same process. The quartz matrices of the mines of the Sierra Nevadas generally contain about 1,000 Troy grains of gold to every 24,000 grains of silver, or about 40 per cent. in value of gold to 60 per cent. in value of silver, and the proportion in other great silver mines of the world varies from 20 to 50 per cent. in value of gold to that of the two metals combined.

Here, then, we have an unalterable reason why all improvements in the art of mining the precious metals must apply equally to both of them, and also why, indeed, so long as one metal is produced, so must be the other. Coupled with that of the relative cost of producing them, as ascertained from an experience of several centuries, this fact assures us not only that 15½ has been the average relation between the metals in the past, but also that it will remain the average relation throughout the future.

The relation being thus fixed, there are powerful influences to keep it there and prevent it from yielding to any temporary vicissitudes, however prolonged, in the supply of the two several metals, such, for example, as the accidental finding of large alluvial deposits or placers of gold, as in the early history of California and Australia. These influences are, first, the vast stock of the precious metals already in existence in the world; and second, the steadying action of the double standard in the countries where it prevails.

I will discuss these two questions in the order named: First, of:

THE WORLD'S STOCK OF THE PRECIOUS METALS.

Estimated stock of the precious metals, in Coin, Plate, &c., in the World at or about the various periods 1803, 1848–'53, *and* 1872.

Period.	Gold.	Silver.	Total.
1803	$1,800,000,000	$3,200,000,000	$5,000,000,000
1848–'53	2,800,000,000	4,000,000,000	6,800,000,000
1872	5,800,000,000	5,600,000,000	11,400,000,000

Estimated stock of the precious metals in Coin in the Occidental or Commercial world at or about the various periods 1803, 1829–'39, 1848–'53, *and* 1872.

Period.	Gold.	Silver.	Total.
1803	$900,000,000	$900,000,000	$1,800,000,000
1829–'39	800,000,000	1,000,000,000	1,800,000,000
1848–'53	1,200,000,000	1,300,000,000	2,500,000,000
1872	2,600,000,000	1,000,000,000	3,600,000,000

Estimated stock of the precious metals, chiefly silver, in Coin in the Oriental or transcommercial world at or about the various periods 1803, 1829–'39, 1848–'53, *and* 1872.

Period.	Stock of coin, chiefly silver.
1803	$700,000,000
1829–'39	800,000,000
1848–'53	900,000,000
1872	2,100,000,000

The above data are derived from a comparison of Ernest Seyd, Wolowski, Jacob, Newmarch, Chevalier, and McCulloch.

INFLUENCE OF THE STOCK OF THE PRECIOUS METALS.

The influence of this stock of the precious metals is perhaps the most important feature of this whole subject, and yet, so far as I am aware, it has either wholly escaped notice or been referred to with but slight appreciation of its consequence.

STEADYING ACTION OF THE DOUBLE STANDARD.

The second great influence which tends to keep steady that relation of 15½ to 1 which the commercial brotherhood of the world and the conditions of the production of the precious metals have primarily occasioned, is the steadying action of the double standard. I can best and most briefly exemplify this action by quoting from Professor Jevons:

"The prices of commodities do not follow the extreme fluctuations of value of both metals as many writers have inconsistently declared. Prices only depend upon the course of the metal which happens to have sunk in value below the legal rates of 15½ to 1, (or whatever else it may be.) Now, if in the accompanying figure we represent by the line A the variation of the value of gold as estimated in terms of some third commodity, say copper, and by the line B the corresponding variations of the value of silver, then superposing these curves, the line C would be the curve expressing the *extreme* fluctuations of both metals. Now, the standard of value always follows the metal which *falls* in value, hence the curve D really shows the course of variation of the standard of value. This line undergoes more frequent undulations than either of the curves of gold or silver, but the fluctuations do not proceed to so great an extent, a point of much greater importance." (W. Stanley Jevons on "Money and the Mechanism of Exchange," N. Y. Appleton, 1875, p. 138.)

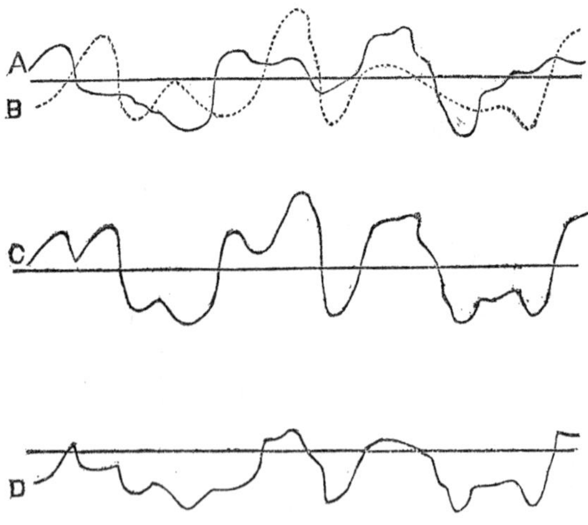

The effect of employing the two metals together is to modify the action of each. Such dual employment prevents one from rising and the other from falling, so that the fluctuations in either "do not proceed to so great an extent" as they otherwise would.

GOLD BY ITSELF NOT A CORRECT MEASURE OF VALUE.

Money is a measure, as the bushel, the rule, and the scale, are measures. The bushel measures capacity, the rule extension, the scale gravity, whilst money measures value. All of these measures are expensive; expensive to produce, expensive to maintain, expensive to preserve. Nor is money by any means the most expensive, it being deemed quite susceptible of demonstration that, compared with the services it performs, it costs even less than the others. Yet, expensive as they are, their use must nevertheless be a source of economy to mankind, or they would certainly not be employed. This employment and the economy to which it is due, ceases, the moment the measures fail of uniformity, definiteness, precision, exactness, and steadiness, for it is in their excellence in these respects that their whole utility resides.

The discordance of moneys, weights, and measures has probably been in all ages one of the first and greatest obstacles which the world's commerce had to overcome, and even the progress of local commerce has had to wait upon uniformity in this respect. Indefinite and unprecise measures are an intolerable evil which men avoid even at the expense of much that is desirable.

What, then, shall be said of measures that are not only discordant and unprecise, but fluctuating also? What would be said of a bushel that alternately contracted and expanded, and contracted more than it expanded; of a rule of elastic rubber, or a pair of scales with a shifting fulcrum? And what shall be said of a fluctuating measure of value?

Yet this is what money is, if gold be regarded to the exclusion of silver.

To be convinced of this it is only necessary to consider the statistics of the precious metals which have just been adduced.

From these tables it will be observed that since nearly the beginning of the present century the stock of coin in the commercial world has exactly doubled, that is to say, it has increased from $1,800,000,000 to $3,600,000,000, an increase that very closely corresponds with population—the population of the Occidental world having been 180,000,000 in 1810 and 360,000,000 in 1875.* Taking both of the precious metals together, the stock of coin has been as nearly as possible $10 per capita of population at each of the four dates mentioned since the beginning of the present century.

At these periods at least, and we have the data for no others, the measure in the commercial world has been apparently unvarying, and this appearance has deceived many writers on the subject; but it is by no means true.

The effective measure of value is not the whole stock of coin, but that portion of it which the law permits to be tendered for the payment of debts. To this should be added the paper substitutes which are from time to time temporarily employed and accepted for the purpose of large payments, and which fluctuate in volume with the vicissitudes of credit and the adoption, transitory operation, and eventual failure of legislative expedients.† The balance of coin or credit no more form a part of the measure of value than do the precious metals when locked up in the form of plate. Now, how much the legal tender coin and substitutes of the commercial world amounted to, at the various dates given, is difficult to estimate. An effort in this direction will, however, be made.

---

*Essay in New York *Independent*, March 11, 1875.

†If legislation were wholly removed from the subject of money except to announce and fix the relation of the metals from time to time, and generally as to police functions, we would have both the metals in circulation plus an amount of free bank paper, which would bear an almost constant relation to the sum of the metals. The measure of value in such case would be easy to ascertain; as it is, nothing is more difficult.

ESTIMATE OF THE EFFECTIVE MEASURE OF VALUE IN 1803.

In 1803, either the single silver, or the double standard prevailed in all the Occidental countries and, except in England, where gold was erroneously overvalued and silver degraded, it was fixed in those countries at such a relation and the coinage of the pieces so arranged (I do not remember having heard of any silver piece heavier than that of two German thalers) as to permit of the employment of nearly the whole mass of silver and gold coin then in the Occident. There was some legal-tender paper or bank paper afloat, notably in England and Russia, which brought the whole amount up to, say $2,000,000,000, with a ratio of activity, let us assume, of 1.

ESTIMATE OF THE EFFECTIVE MEASURE OF VALUE IN 1872.

In 1872 a single gold standard existed in Great Britain; a restricted double standard in the Latin countries; a single silver standard in other European countries; a disused double standard in the United States and legal-tender paper notes in many of these countries. The sum of all these currencies might amount to $4,000,000,000, with a ratio of activity of, say 2, making $8,000,000,000 in 1872, with a population of 360,000,000, or $22 *per capita*, as against $2,000,000,000 in 1803, with a population of 180,000,000, or, $11 *per capita.* The effective measure of value in the Occidental world has, therefore, doubled, since the beginning of this century.

As it is worth while to ascertain, if possible, how we may obtain a least varying measure of value for the world it becomes necessary for this purpose to turn from the statistics of the Occidental world to those of the whole world.

THE WORLD'S STOCK OF COIN AND POPULATION.

Assuming that without royal, seigniorial, or legislative interference, the relation of the mass of private credit current for money, to the mass of money, would be constant, let us confine our observation to the stock of metal money in the World. In 1803, with a population of, say 900,000,000, it was $2,500,000,000; in 1829, with a population of, say 1,000,000,000, it was $2,600,000,000; in 1848–53, with a population of, say 1,100,000,000, it was $3,400,000,000; and in 1872, with a population of, say, 1,200,000,000,* it was $5,700,000,000.

SWELLING OF THE MEASURE OF VALUE SINCE 1803.

These figures give an average of coin *per capita* throughout the world amounting to $2.83, $2.60, $3.09, and $4.75, at the respective periods named. If the assumptions of population here employed are admitted to be even approximately correct, then, even without reckoning the greater activity of money now than formerly, it would follow that there has been no more fixedness in the relation of the World's coin and population than there has been in that of the effective measure of value and population of the Occident. They have both doubled, or about doubled, since the beginning of the century—doubled *per capita* of population. The coin of the world *per capita* and the effective measure of value of the Occident *per capita* (*i. e.*, the coin and circulating credit of the Occident combined) have both doubled.

What has caused this doubling, this unsteadiness of the measure of value? Has it been due to diminution in the population of the world? No. We know that the population of the Occidental world has more than doubled since the beginning of the century, while the figures assumed for the Oriental world exhibit a very small increase.†

---

* Behm and Wagner sum up the population of the world for 1872 at 1,391,000,000, but in this they include China at 446,000,000. There is no authority for this extravagant figure besides that of the Chinese mandarin's communication to Lord Macartney in 1795. It was therein stated at 333,000,000, which was probably excessive by more than one-half. Consult the numerous and much more reliable estimates in Malte-Brun's Geography.

† Japan increases very slightly. As to India and China, they are probably stationary.

Has it been due to superabundance in the stock of silver? No. That stock was $1,600,000,000 in 1803; $1,800,000,000 in 1829; $2,200,000,000 in 1848, and $3,100,000,000 in 1872. Its ratio to population has been, as the ratio of money to population always should be, a slightly increasing one; but the relation has been substantially constant.

THE MEASURE OF VALUE SWOLLEN BY GOLD.

The swelling of the measure of value has been due to an enormous increase in the stock of gold. This amounted to $1,800,000,000 in 1803, and twenty-six years afterwards it had not increased. During the next nineteen years it increased 50 per cent., and during the following twenty-four years it increased 116 per cent. over the previous increase. In 1848 it was $1,200,000,000, in 1872 it was $2,600,000,000; by the end of the present century it will probably have fallen again to $2,200,000,000, perhaps to $2,000,000,000. So much for a metal which depends upon placer mining for its chief supplies.

This is the steady and unvarying measure of value to which the advocates of the single gold standard would commit us!

So far as steadiness is concerned, and irrespective of all other considerations, gold does not deserve to be used as money at all, and the old nations of Asia, who tried this metal more than thirty centuries ago, appear to have long since come to this conclusion; but the gradual increase of the mass of silver and the weight of the coins, together with the fact that gold frequently occurs with silver in the same matrix, give a place to gold which the unsteadiness of its supply would otherwise deny to it.

ANNUAL PRODUCTION OF GOLD AND SILVER SEPARATELY.

The validity of the statistics which have been quoted rests upon authorities—Wolowski, Seyd, Chevalier, McCulloch, and Jacob—whom the reading world has thus far been satisfied to accept as safe guides. The important and conclusive deductions drawn from them are, however, not without an amplitude of other support. They are to be drawn also from the statistics of the annual production of the precious metals, the validity of which will admit of but little question.

Estimated annual production of the precious metals throughout the entire world (exclusive of India, China, and Japan) at various periods during the nineteenth century. Sums in millions of dollars and tenths.*

Period.	*Gold.*	*Silver.*	*Total.*	*Authority.*
1800†	–	36.3	49.3	Phillips.
1801	13.0	–		Birkmyre.
1829	5.0	20.0	25.0	Estimate based on McCulloch.‡
1846§	29.2	32.5	61.7	McCulloch's Dic. of Commerce.
1848	67.5	–	–	Westminster Review, Jan., 1876.
1850‖	93.2	43.9	137.1	McCulloch.
1851	120.0	–	–	Westminster Review, Jan., 1876.
1852	182.5	40.5	223.0	Journ. des Economistes, Mar '76.
1852	193.7	–	–	Westminster Review, Jan., 1876.
1853	155.0	40.5	195.5	Journal des Economistes.
1853	–	–	160.0	Blake.
1854	–	47.4	–	Whitney, by countries, App. Cycl., XV, 53, new edition.

*No mines in India. (McCulloch in Encyc. Brit. Ed., 1858, p. 470.) Gold mines in China, but not worked (472) for the reason, according to Sir R. Murchison, that it would conflict with Chinese theory relative to maintaining "balance of the circulating medium." Otreschoff estimated total yield of precious metals in China, India, Japan, &c., in 1854 at $30,000,000 a year, but this is evidently too high. Whitney estimates the gold product of all Southern Asia at $600,000 a year. Perhaps, in view of Newmarch's statement, (Tooke, vi, 723,) that the specie (coin, trinkets, &c.,) in India amounts to £400,000,000, of which say one-half is in coin, and allowing same for China and Japan, total coin in Southern Asia $2,000,000,000—the total product of Southern Asia may be approximately as follows: Silver 29, gold 1, total 30. Allowing one and a half per cent. per annum for wear and loss of coin, it would require at least this amount to keep up the stock, while European and American supplies would be needed for the arts and to make provision for increasing population. Adding these sums to the above estimate for 1874 we have the following grand total annual production for the entire world—sums in millions of dollars:

1874.	Gold.	Silver.	Total.
The world exclusive of Southern Asia	90.5	71.5	162.0
Southern Asia	1.0	29.0	30.0
	91.5	100.5	192.0

† Estimated by Raymond (Rep. of 1875) 15 gold and 40 silver; but this estimate, though not very wide of the mark, is without authority. Phillips gives details by countries.

‡ McCulloch states (and in this he agrees with all other authors) that the lowest point of production was reached in 1829. He states that Mexico and South America together only produced of both metals $20,000,000, chiefly silver, and that very little was elsewhere produced. Allowing $5,000,000 for what was elsewhere produced, crediting that $5,000,000 to silver and allowing one-fourth of the American product to have been in gold, (which exceeds the proportion estimated by Jacob for the same period,) I accord to silver $20,000,000 and to gold $5,000,000.

§ Estimated by Raymond at 43 gold and 39 silver; but wide of the mark and without authority. Birkmyre gives details by countries for 31.5 silver.

‖ For about this date DeBow, ii, 558, gives $131,500,000, gold and silver, as follows:

California	£14,500,000
Brazil	7,000,000
Russia	3,350,000
Great Britain (silver)	50,000
Asia	1,400,000
$131,500,000	£26,300,000

Phillips gives details for 43.8 silver. (App. Cyc. xv, 53.)

Estimated annual production, &c—Continued.

Period.	*Gold.*	*Silver.*	*Total.*	*Authority.*
1854	127.0	40.5	167.5	Journal des Economistes.
1855	135.0	40.5	175.5	Ibid.
1856	147.5	40.5	188.0	Ibid.
1857	133.0	40.5	173.5	Ibid.
1857	–	–	195.0	McCulloch.
1858	124.5	40.5	165.0	Journal des Economistes.
1859	124.5	40.5	165.0	Ibid.
1860	119.0	40.5	159.5	Ibid.
1861	114.0	42.5	156.5	Ibid.
1861	–	56.0	–	Soetbeer.
1862	107.5	45.0	152.5	Journal des Economistes.
1863	107.0	49.0	156.0	Ibid.
1864	113.0	51.5	164.5	Ibid.
1865	120.0	52.0	172.0	Ibid.
1865	130.7	62.3	193.0	Blake for gold, 1867; Phillips for silver, 1865.
1866	121.0	50.5	171.5	Journal des Economistes.
1867	–	53.8	–	Blake, by countries, App. Cyc., XV, 53, new edition.
1867	116.0	54.0	170.0	Journal des Economistes.
1868	120.0	50.0	170.0	Ibid.
1869	121.0	47.5	168.5	Ibid.
1870	116.0	51.5	167.5	Ibid.
1871	116.5	61.0	177.5	Ibid.
1872	101.5	65.0	166.5	Ibid.
1873	103.5	70.0	173.5	Ibid.
1873	103.5	76.3	179.8	Ibid. for gold, App. Cyc. for silv.
1874	90.5	71.5	162.0	Journal des Economistes.
1875	97.5	62.0	159.5	Ibid.
1875	118.0	72.0	190.0	Estimate.*

Taking silver by itself, we find that the annual production of the Occidental world has but little more than kept pace with population. It was $35,000,000 a year at about the beginning of the century; it was $72,000,000 a year in 1875. The statistics of its annual production are characterized by the same steadiness that distinguishes its place in the circulation. If gentlemen want details they can have them country by country. There is no guess work here; we are standing upon solid rock.

Turning to gold we find that the annual production has varied enormously. It was $13,000,000 a year in 1801; fell to perhaps not over $5,000,000 in 1829; rose to $182,-500,000 in 1852; fell to $107,000,000 in 1863; rose to

*The French estimate is considered to be at least $10,000,000 too low for silver. Silver in the United States for 1875 was $25,000,000 more than in 1868. The French estimate is also believed to be too low for gold.

$130,000,000 in 1865, and fell to $97,500,000 in 1875, and with a downward tendency.

And yet this wildly fluctuating, ruinously unsteady metal is what the fledglings of political economy, the charlatans of monetary conventions, and the numerous other dupes of Lombard street would divorce from its natural complement, silver, and have for a sole standard of value. As well have the rack for a measure. It has often served that purpose, only the thing that it measured was not value, but human endurance, and that seems to be about all that gold by itself is capable of measuring. Thirteen million dollars a year in 1801; $5,000,000 in 1829; $182,000,000 in 1852; $97,500,000 in 1875; a wonderful measure of value indeed!

Let us suppose for a moment that silver had been demonetized by the entire commercial world at the same time that England demonetized it, to wit, in 1816, and the commerce, the business, and the vested interests, the daily labor and the time contracts of society, left to adjust themselves in the course of twenty-six years (from 1803 to 1829) from a measure of $1,800,000,000 of gold and silver coin, to one of, say, $700,000,000 or $800,000,000 of gold coin! Recollect that even as it was, the whole of that period was one of bankruptcies and convulsions. Now, let me ask what it would have been, had the evil been aggravated by the adoption of such a gigantic blunder as England set up in 1816 for the imitation of mankind?

We are upon the eve of another era of the same character. The annual supply of gold has reached its culmination. The supplies of gold are falling off. The river beds of California and Australia have been washed; the surface gold has been secured; the quartz mines have measuredly used up the paying ore; the water-line has been touched, and below it are only those sulphurets which as yet have not been successfully treated. Beware foreign influence! Beware the example of England! Beware England's fatal blunder of 1816! Beware the ruinous effects that followed close upon its heels! The causes of the bankruptcies of 1873, 1874, 1875, and 1876 may lie in deeper waters than the shallow stream which commenced to flow in October, 1873. They may lie in the shrinkage of gold—that gold which the ill-considered act of 1873 made the sole measure of values and the sole arbiter of fortunes in the United States.

For the purpose of testing by comparison the efficiency of gold as a measure of values, let us suppose again that gold was the sole legal tender money of the commercial world in 1848. Will gentlemen attempt to deny that the stock of this metal in the coins of the commercial world more than doubled between that date and 1867? If this fact be admitted, must it not be perceived that, with gold as the sole standard of value, prices would have more than doubled during the course of these nineteen years, and that with such a great and sudden enhancement of prices the worth of all vested interests, the relations of all contracts, the entire distribution of wealth, would have been seriously affected? The widow and the orphan, left with a comfortable competence in 1848, might have had to eke out a scanty living in 1867; the lessor of 1848 might have been glad to abandon his property rather than pay the taxes and charges of 1867; the rich would have become undeservedly poor, and the poor undeservedly rich—a very equitable arrangement, according to some minds, and I confess I am not wholly unbiased that way myself; but I do not forget that I am now addressing the official successors of the authors of the act of 1873.

Observe, too, the effect which the enormous folly of demonetizing silver in certain States of Europe and in the United States has had upon the currency of Asia. If these statistics have even approximate worth, and there is no reason to subject them to the slightest suspicion of incorrectness, for they rest upon numerous authorities who derived their data from widely-different sources, it will be seen that the currency of Asia has more than doubled since 1848, and probably chiefly since 1862. This currency is estimated to have amounted to $700,000,000 in 1803, $900,000,000 in 1848, and $2,100,000,000 in 1872, chiefly in silver. So far as we know, and are led to believe, from the character and institutions of the peoples of these countries, there was little or no increase at all in their numbers up to 1862, if, indeed, there has been any since that date. The increase of their circulating medium has, therefore, been almost absolute, and it must have had the effect of enhancing the present level of prices in those countries three times more than that of 1803.

No wonder that Mr. Secretary Bristow advises Congress that the abolition of our import duty upon tea has failed to cheapen the price of that article. Why we should have contributed, as we did contribute, by the suspension act of 1862 and the demonetization act of 1873, to triple the specie prices of everything we have had, and shall have, to buy, from China, Japan, and the East Indies, wholly surpasses the understanding. To men of plain minds it seems to have been the most stupendous folly.

APOLOGIES FOR SUBSIDIARY COINAGE.

To these grave charges about tripling prices in Asia there has been a weak and ill-considered reply, to the effect that while England and her subservient imitators on the continent of Europe and in this country have demonetized silver, as a legal tender for the payment of debts, that metal has, nevertheless, been allowed to remain in the form of base coin for fractional currency or small change. It seems to have been forgotten that base or token money can only circulate to a small amount. For example, if gold and silver were now equally legal tender in Great Britain, as they were previous to 1717, a large proportion, perhaps one-half, of the whole amount of money now in the kingdom, which is estimated at $575,000,000, (plus $5,000,000 of copper,) would be of silver, which, at the present moment, is the cheaper metal, at the relation of 15½. In France, in 1860, where the double standard prevailed, and when gold was the cheaper metal, at the legal relation of 15½, a large portion of the entire metallic currency was of gold.* But instead of the currency of England being entirely of silver, at the present time there are in that country $500,000,000 of gold and only $75,000,000 of silver (tokens) in circulation.† This result is due to the demonetization of silver, and from this cause some $200,000,000 of silver, which would otherwise hold place in the money of that country, have either been melted up or exported; reduced either to plate or shipped to Asia; in the one case lost almost irretrievably to civilization, so far as its agency in measuring values and stimulating industry is concerned; in the other gone to help add to the strength and commercial resources of a semi-barbarous world.

But far more important than this is the consideration that the substance of which coins are made and the substance of which the standard is composed are altogether different matters. The coins of a country may be made of gold or silver; yet if wheat were made the standard of value, that is to say, if the coins were payable on demand in wheat, the prices of other commodities would fluctuate not with the vicissitudes of coinage nor even of the stock and production of the precious metals, but with those of the stock and production of wheat. Coins of this character would merely be tokens, promises to pay (wheat) stamped on gold or silver; of this character are the silver coins of England, and the silver half dollars, quarters, and dimes of the United States. They are mere tokens, and, except at times when they rose in value (in the standard) so as to be worth melting or exporting, the metal of which they were composed would practically be demonetized.

SUBSIDIARY COINAGE NOT WHAT IS WANTED.

It is not merely urged by the advocates of the double standard that silver should have that subordinate place in the currency which is the utmost that can be filled by a token coinage, and which could be filled to a certain extent as well

---

*Seyd. †Jevons.

by any baser metal or even perhaps by paper; it is not merely asked that silver shall be granted the same sort of recognition that is vouchsafed in social life to a menial; it is demanded that it shall be accorded the same rank in which gold has been maintained; the rank to which the great place of silver in the coins of the world, its universal distribution and appreciation, its ample and steady supply, its twin-birth, its utility and adaptability, and its worth as a measure of value, entitle it. With a double standard wisely fixed, all the moderately large payments would be made in gold and all the smaller ones in silver, just as for moderately large quantities of liquids the oaken hogshead is employed, and for smaller ones, the tin gallon. By forcibly interdicting oak you might compel hogsheads to be measured by the tin gallon, just as by interdicting tin you might force gallons to be measured by the oaken hogshead. What is demanded for silver is that it shall be left free to assume its own rank in the currency, so that whenever it temporarily becomes the cheaper metal at the average relation to gold, it may for the time possess that same influence in modifying the measure of value that has been always so zealously accorded to it when it became the dearer.

THE FLUCTUATIONS IN GOLD DUE CHIEFLY TO PLACER MINING.

It will not do to rejoin to this that the probabilities of gold again becoming the metal in more plentiful supply, are remote. Even if true, this reply would confess the very selfishness of the champions of the gold standard which they have been so solicitious to conceal in the solemnity of their monetary conventions and the surreptitious character of their measures of legislation. But it is not true. Although at the present time the annual supplies of gold are falling off, it is impossible to predict how long this movement may last. While silver is essentially the product of industry and enterprise, gold is largely that of adventure and chance. This results from the physical fact that the last named metal is nearly always found in alluvial deposits or placers, and it is from these sources that the bulk of the world's stock of gold has been obtained; this is never the case with silver.

GOLD AT PRESENT CHIEFLY A BRITISH PRODUCT.

These facts bring under our consideration another important matter in connection with the history of the precious metals separately. It is this: that at the present time and for the main part the supplies of gold to the world are chiefly from British countries or countries subject to British domination. The following table will illustrate this very significant statement:

Estimated annual gold product of the world at latest dates for which the statistics are attainable in the various official reports.

The United States, 1875		$26,000,000
Australia, etc., 1872	$58,000,000	
British Columbia	2,000,000	
Canada and Nova Scotia	500,000	
Other British Possessions and British isles	1,500,000	
Total British Possessions		62,000,000
Balance of the world		30,000,000
Total world		$118,000,000
Proportion of the world's production from British Possessions (per cent)		52½

From this table it will be observed that of the $118,000,000, which represent the annual gold product of the world 52½ per cent. was obtained in countries over which the British flag waved or which were subject to British domination.

Is this, then, the secret of British plutocratical solicitude for the single gold standard? Is it not only that the people of Great Britain shall have the rewards of their labor measured by this diminishing measure, which is to be held tightly grasped in the monopolizing and cruel hands of their plutocratic lords, but that the labor of the entire civilized world shall be measured by it also? For one, I reply to this, never! And when this subject shall be fully understood by the American people, the reply that I now make should echo and reverberate throughout the whole length and breadth of this great land. Never ought we, never will we, submit to have our labor and enterprise measured by a standard subject to the manipulation and pleasure of a foreign nation, and of a class hostile to the genius of our institutions.

THE DOUBLE STANDARD FOR THE UNITED STATES.

Hitherto the double standard has been alluded to with reference to its great superiority as a measure of value for the exchanges of the world. I now propose to treat it solely or chiefly with reference to the affairs of the United States.

Many of the considerations adverted to in connection with its superiority as a measure of value for all nations apply with equal, and sometimes more than equal, force to this nation. Briefly recapitulated they are mainly as follows:

The convenience of employing gold for moderately large payments and of silver for smaller ones induces both metals to be employed as money, whether one or the other, or both or neither, are made the standard of value. The violent aberrations in the annual supplies of gold, the steadiness of silver, the often deficient and sometimes excessive supplies of the one, and the always ample supplies of the other, forbid us to rely upon one as a standard of value to the exclusion of the other, and particularly when that one is gold. And this objection to gold as the sole standard of value obtains additional force at a time like the present, when its annual supply is diminishing every year, its distribution throughout the world is narrowing, and its production is at the mercy of the arms and legislation of a single powerful nation and a class hostile to the growth and prosperity of republican communities.

Another basic consideration is the stock of precious

metals in possession of the world, the product of many centuries of toil, abstinence, contention, suffering, and sacrifice. It is this stock which measures prices. Nearly one-half of it consists of silver. To demonetize this half will reduce all prices one-half and convulse every country in the world, except those which may refuse to take part in such demonetization.

Beyond these considerations, however, there are others which apply with peculiar force to the present time and to our own country. These will be treated in their proper order.

EFFECTS UPON THE DEBTOR AND CREDITOR CLASSES.

First, with regard to the effect of the standard on the debtor and creditor classes.

At the outset, let it be premised to the great honor and glory of our country that, in the sense in which the term is used in England, we have no debtor and creditor classes. Notwithstanding the tendency of the national debt and of the other financial scars which the recent great civil conflict has left upon the war-worn features of the nation, we have no permanent debtors and creditors. The man who is a debtor to-day becomes a creditor to-morrow, and the creditor of to-morrow becomes the debtor of next day after to-morrow. We are all in the same boat in this country: all struggling, toiling, risking, winning, or losing. There are no hereditary privileges, no entailed estates, no permanently vested interests. Misadventure, death, unexpected legislation, in a word, a thousand agencies, are continually at work to redistribute wealth and redistribute poverty; whilst a free soil, boundless natural resources, thoroughly diffused and abundant education, and a universal spirit of enterprise, contribute to increase our stock of wealth; so that while the gifts of fortune are being continually redistributed, those of intelligence and industry, which are always fairly distributed at the outset, are being added to them—an equalizing reservoir with an already equalized and always rising level.

Therefore, the remarks which will now be devoted to the consideration of the respective equities of the debtor and creditor classes will apply with far less cogency to the affairs of this country than to those of any other.

It was not complained by the debtor class, when the act of 1873 was passed, that it would tend to favor the interests of the creditor class, as it undoubtedly did. Why was no complaint made? Because the act was so drawn that it apparently related only to the technical regulation of the mints, and gave no notice, either from its title or its text, that that far graver measure—a change of the standard of value—was proposed. There is no mention of the term "standard of value" in the act; there is not even mention made of the silver legal tender dollar which the act abolished. None but those fully conversant with the history of our legislation upon the subject of money, none but those who were familiar with the details and principles of the long-forgotten act of 1792 and subsequent legislation, could have understood the full purport of the important changes of legislation which the passage of the act of 1873 involved.

Moreover, specie payments had been suspended for eleven years, nor, for more than two years afterward, was there any provision made for resumption, and resumption appeared so far off in 1872, that is to say, at the time the Demonetization Act was introduced into Congress, that the effects of demonetization, coupled with those of resumption, were not realized or anticipated. The silver dollar had not been coined at our mints for many years, and during the fall of gold subsequent to 1848 had gone out of circulation, except for the payment of ground-rents in Philadelphia and elsewhere, and for the purposes of the Asiatic trade. The demonetization of the silver dollar at such a period was, like a stab in the dark, unexpected, unseen, and not to be felt until too late to be averted.

There was, therefore, no notice to the debtor class, who are always the poorer class, and, therefore, the more numerous and widespread, the least organized, the least protected by the law, the least courted by ambition or favored by power.

In the absence of such complaint from the debtors in 1873, in the absence of any notice which was practically accessible to them of the supernal importance of the change proposed, what right would now the creditor class possess to object to the rehabilitation and restoration of the double standard? Clearly none whatever.

I do not speak now of the creditors of the Government, whose status in respect of the coin in which their claims are to be paid is not proposed to be discussed; I speak of creditors generally. In view of the concealed effects of the demonetization act of 1873, in view of the fact that resumption was not provided for until 1875, in view of the utter absence of complaint from the debtor class when the demonetization act was passed, what right or even shadow of right has any class of creditors now to object to the monetization of the silver dollar? The Demonetization Act was not passed at their solicitation any more than it was passed with the knowledge or concurrence of the debtors. It was not a contract between the Government and the people. It was a mere caprice of legislation, which could be undone, which, in deference to public policy and justice, should be undone, and which, under our organic law, which, as I hope presently to show, raises the double standard far above the province of legislation, must be undone.

But putting all this aside and looking at the question purely as an economical and political one, and without reference either to its merits or its history, both of which so emphatically decide in favor of the double standard, let us see which class it is that, when benefits or advantages are to be dispensed, a wise and particularly a republican Government should favor.

Is it the creditor class, who consist to some extent of capitalists whose estates were hereditary, of others whose estates were the result of chance, unexpected death, unlooked-for legislation, or extraordinary and unforeseeable events? Is it the creditor class, whose garnered capital represents the results of past labor, perhaps of that of the serf, the slave, the overworked, browbeaten, fagged and famished victim of toil? Is it the creditor class, who are always allied to an effete conservatism, out of which spring caste and aristocracy and feudal privileges and every other odious form of power, to whom legislative favors shall be granted? Is it the creditor class, who least stand in need of such favors or advantages?

To whom shall legislation dispense what small favors it may have to bestow in a country so free and republican as this? Shall it be to the class whose tendencies I have depicted or to the debtor class, to the poor, the needy, the temporarily depressed, the cast-down, the struggling, the toiling, the enterprising, the active, the aspiring, the ever hopeful?

Shall the favors of legislation be granted to those who ask for them and fawn and intrigue for them, or to those who never ask, nor fawn, nor intrigue?

Shall they be granted to those whom we here in Congress do not represent, or to those whom we do?

Shall they be awarded to the many whose servants we are, or to the few whose servants we are not? For remember that this is a Government based upon numbers and not upon wealth, and that the States and Commonwealths which are represented in this Chamber are also based upon the principle of numbers, of the greatest good to the greatest number.

If there are favors to be accorded, let the People have them. It is upon *their* prosperity and welfare that this country, nay the entire world, essentially depends for its advancement; not upon the patronage of a class.

NO ADVANTAGES TO BE GAINED BY EITHER CLASS.

But I deny that there are any favors or advantages to be granted by a return to the double standard. A single standard confers advantages, advantages to the few, whilst a double standard divides and distributes advantages. This is fully illustrated by Professor Jevon's diagram. The double standard both gives and takes. It strikes a medium between the metals, although but one of them may chiefly be employed in the currency, and that, the one of temporarily the lesser purchasing power. There is no practical difference between its effects and those which would flow from the adoption of a single metal which is adhered to as the standard forever, a metal which is always in as sufficient supply, and as widely distributed and largely held as now are both the metals combined, provided such a metal could be found. And whatever infinitessimally small difference there is, whatever poor crumb of advantage the restoration of the double standard would afford to the debtor class, it bears no comparison at all with the full ration, the stuffed loaf of advantage which the continuation of the single gold standard is destined to confer upon the creditor class, while the annual supplies of gold are diminishing in quantity. Whatever advantage there was in the double standard, if it was worth the planning of one class to destroy it, it is due to the interests of the other and the welfare of the nation to restore it.

Moreover, and from a higher point of view, it is in the long run really to the interest of the creditor class, as well as of that larger class who are neither creditors nor debtors, for us to restore the double standard. It is to the interest of honor, of virtue, of religion, of good-will to all men and peace upon earth. It will tend to save the debtor from despair and the resources which despair invites; from dishonest bankruptcy, from flight, from the sequestration of property, from its malicious and revengeful destruction, from popular agitation, agrarian disturbances, and revolution, and from recourse to "interchangeable bonds" or other covert forms of repudiation.

I have said that the practical effects of the double standard would be like that of a single metal which is adhered to forever. I meant by this that a single metal adhered to forever would have its ups as well as downs, as England has had with gold since 1816. It was down with the people of that country until about the year 1832 or 1837, then slowly up until 1848, then rapidly up until 1865, and since that year slowly down. With a double standard, England would have had fewer of these vicissitudes; with the restoration of our double standard we shall have fewer of them than otherwise. These vicissitudes are clearly traceable to those disturbances of the double standard which commenced in 1816. They are still unsettled. With their settlement, with the return of nations to that dual employment of gold and silver which was never interrupted until England saw fit to interrupt it, will doubtless return that era of monetary ease and serenity which characterized the last century, during which the Bank of England rate scarcely varied one-half of one per cent. Bank panics and financial revulsions will disappear, and possibly also the thousand and one mad schemes of irredeemable paper which necessity and despair have driven men to entertain.

But a single standard adhered to forever is something that even were a steady enough and otherwise suitable metal obtainable for the purpose—which is absolutely denied—is not to be looked for. It is true that England adhered to gold all through that period so trying to her plutocratical rulers, from 1848 to 1865, but it was not without having often been on the point of abolishing it and resorting to some substance for money the supplies of which did not increase so rapidly. The propositions of Cobden and some of the other writers I have quoted, in favor of adopting wheat, &c., as standards of value, sufficiently attest the alarm of the ruling classes. But, fortunately for the people of England, the popular sufferings of the previous period from 1816 to 1830, when gold was yearly diminishing in supply, had gone far enough to produce the reaction which the short-sighted and selfish adoption of the gold standard so richly merited. A stern remembrance of these sufferings was abroad in the land, and forbade any further tampering with the standard. The people said in effect—said it in the Chartist and the Anti-Corn Law, and the Reform contentions—it was your turn a while since, it is ours now; stand back and let's have fair play! The yeomanry of England had arisen from its pauper grave and the voice of power trembled, and was hushed in its presence.

While these circumstances forbade the desertion of that standard which the plutocracy of 1816 had set up for itself, there is no assurance that they would not again be evoked to prevent a change of the standard from gold to silver should the latter once more become the dearer metal. The plutocracy of England found strong enough arguments to change the standard from the double to the single and from silver to gold. The plutocracies of the Continental countries have changed from one metal to the other whenever it suited, or they fancied it suited, their present interest most. Neither, with the increasing advantages and power which the retention of the gold standard would confer upon our rising and promising regiments of plutocrats, would this class fail to make similar attempts in this country, and particularly if the easy success they met with in 1873 is suffered to stand unrebuked. In effect, the standard would be changed whenever there occurred a marked change in the values of the metals.

We should have a double standard, indeed; only, instead of standing upon two supports it would rest upon one. Instead of having its center of gravity always midway between its supports it would have one that rocked to and fro, and at every oscillation tore away a portion of those foundations of equity upon which alone republican institutions and republican government may permanently rest.

RESORT TO A GOLD STANDARD INEVITABLY INVITES PAPER INFLATIONS.

An extremely important consideration has been adverted to, and demands some elaboration. It is this: that any attempt to substitute by force of law, gold for silver, in the money of a country, at a time when gold is becoming scarcer, either absolutely or relatively as to silver, must surely result in producing paper inflations. Paper notes, either representative or unrepresentative, are sure to be issued as substitutes for gold as it becomes scarce. Any attempt to artificially enhance the purchasing power of gold, either by demonetizing or partly demonetizing silver, and the act of 1873 is of this nature, is certain to invite or prolong the issuance of paper notes. By artificially enhancing the purchasing power of gold, the profits arising from the issuance of paper notes are enhanced, and the pressure on the part of banks and individuals to obtain authority to issue them, if, indeed, the decline of prices and consequent stagnation of industry does not induce the Government itself to issue them, will become too great to be successfully resisted. This authority once obtained, or this power once exercised, it always proceeds to extremes. Neither reason nor prudence sets a limit to the emission of paper notes; the emission usually continues until it ends in general bankruptcy.

This, then, is what the purblind, short-sighted advocates of a single metal, when both metals together are barely more than sufficient to prevent the world's stock of coin from falling behind the increase of population, this, is what they would invite. They would press the blade down to the point at which it is bound to spring up—spring up in defective and excessive credit, in speculation, in madness, in bankruptcy, and in crime. They would twist the thumb-screw down until the debtor was reduced to poverty and despair, forgetting that they themselves, more than any class of persons, were interested in keeping him solvent and prosperous.

The lesson is the same in all artificial or forced systems of currency. Money came into existence freely, and it has never yet yielded up its birthright. Legislation should not, legislation *cannot* enthrall it. Beyond the scope of temporarily fixing the relation, which should be the mean natural or market relation, between two metals, both of which are indispensable for the purposes of exchange;

beyond manufacturing and unitizing coins, and punishing counterfeitors; in short, beyond the exercise of that surveillance, which may fitly be termed the police of money, legislation has neither rightful function nor power. All it can do beyond this is to confuse, to deceive to injure, to disturb, and to invite loss, discontent, turbulence, violence, and anarchy.

Gentlemen may fancy that they are playing upon a very simple instrument when they undertake to meddle with money. But they are mistaken. The apparently simple instrument is an organism of the most complex character, the result of thirty centuries of growth and development, and like all highly-developed organisms, impatient of control or restraint. It recoils from the first touch of an unaccustomed hand; it gives forth alarming sounds; and if further meddled with, it revenges itself upon its disturber with overwhelming ruin.

DANGER OF ABANDONING THE DOUBLE STANDARD.

It is impossible to resume specie payments in gold alone. Let us try to grasp the full significance of this proposition, if even it be only in one respect—that of the capacity of the mines of the world to supply it with gold enough to measure its exchanges without the co-ordinate employment of silver. Given bills of exchange, given certificates of deposit, given bank-bills, given government legal-tender notes, given railways, telegraphs—in short, any form of representative or non-representative money or of agencies for increasing the rapidity of its circulation—given all these, and the world now employs them all whenever and wheresoever they can be employed with safety or advantage, and often when neither one nor the other is secured; given all these, and yet a certain quantity of the precious metals is needed at bottom, as the foundation upon which the entire basis of credit, safe and unsafe, must rest. Now, how much does this indispensable quantity of the precious metals amount to at the present time?

There is no difficulty in answering this question. The

world's stock of coin is $5,700,000,000, of which nearly one-half is of silver. Of this sum Europe, America, and the rest of the Occidental world employ about $3,600,000,000. Previous to the late partial demonetizations of silver in the Latin Union, and in Germany and the United States, these $3,600,000,000 consisted of, let us say, $2,000,000,000 of gold and $1,600,000,000 of silver. They now consist of say about $2,400,000,000 gold and $1,200,000,000 silver. By continuing to exclude silver from equal participation with gold in the currency of the United States, and attempting to resume specie payments, we occasion a demand for say $350,000,000 of gold wherewith to pay off the greenbacks and furnish bank reserves and $50,000,000 of silver in lieu of the fractional notes. If we could obtain these $400,000,000 of metal without drawing it from other countries in Europe or America, they would add so much to the stock of coin in the Occidental world, which would then be $2,750,000,000 of gold and $1,250,000,000 of silver. This is the answer to the question so far as the Occidental world is concerned. The quantity of the precious metals needed for money and the basis of credit in the Occidental world—that is to say, the quantity needed to maintain prices at their present level—is at least $4,000,000,000. Of this sum the United States, if it succeeds in resuming specie payments, will hold about $400,000,000.

Now, let me ask, in the first place, where these $400,000,000 are expected to come from? Gentlemen may dispute the premiss and contend that no such sum as $400,000,000 is necessary. They may point to the fact that just previous to the time of the suspension in 1862 the entire stock of coin in this country was estimated at not over $300,000,000,* of which probably not over three-fourths or $225,000,000 were in gold. Granted that this was the fact, and I have no doubt it was, it must not be forgotten that since 1862 the population of this country has increased 50 per cent., and its exchanges fully 100 per cent. What is the proof of this?

*Finance Report, 1861, pp. 25 and 62.

Simply that in 1861 our whole circulating media consisted of $300,000,000 in coin and $200,000,000 of bank notes, which circulated within limited areas at or nearly par; whereas, now it consists of not more than $140,000,000 of coin and some $750,000,000 of Government and bank paper, the latter circulating (throughout nearly the whole country) at about 87½ cents to the dollar; say total circulation at par equal to $800,000,000. This is 70 per cent. more than the par circulation of 1861; an incontestable proof that exchanges have increased in volume at least 70 per cent. Taking into consideration the superior activity of the legal tender and national bank notes over the old State bank notes, and the improvement and development of railways, telegraphs, clearing houses, and other mechanisms of exchange, since 1861, it cannot be doubted that the bulk of to-day's exchanges in this country is at least double that of a corresponding day in 1862. Suppose, however, we put it at only 70 per cent. higher: then, in order to resume specie payment upon at least as firm a footing as specie payments stood in 1861—and the universal suspension of the banks toward the end of that year proves that it was not so firm a footing as could have been wished—we shall require at least 70 per cent. more specie than we employed in 1861. Add 70 per cent. to $300,000,000, and you have $510,000,000. Allow $140,000,000 for specie already in the country, in the banks, in private hands, and in the vaults of the Treasury, and you will need $370,000,000 in order to resume. Of this $370,000,000 the Government will need, perhaps, about $350,000,000, and the banks the remainder. But the apportionment is of no consequence in this connection. The substantial fact is that in order to resume specie payments we shall need $370,000,000, say, for round figures, $400,000,000, of specie, of which, under the operation of the act of 1873, about $350,000,000 must be in gold.

I now ask where are these $350,000,000 expected to come from? Again, do I fancy I hear interpellation. I shall perhaps be told that a proposition is even now before Congress, a proposition from careful and able sources, and boasting the indorsement of high financial authority, a proposition which assumes that $100,000,000 in gold will be sufficient wherewith to enable the country to return to specie payments.

I refer to a speech which has been made in the Senate. But I warn gentlemen to beware of making a mistake in respect of this matter, for a mistake will set us back many years. The British Government tried to resume in 1817, after a suspension of twenty years, but it failed, and resumption was deferred for seven other years, until 1824. If we try to resume in 1879 with $100,000,000 and fail, we may be set back a quarter of a century. Moreover, if we fail, somebody—most probably some clique of stock gamblers—will make fifteen or twenty per cent. out of the operation. How? Easy enough! Knowing that $100,000,000 was the limit of the Government's ability to pay, they could easily make arrangements with the banks and depositories throughout the country to withdraw $100,000,000 of greenbacks on the eve of the day of resumption, and present them for payment at the Treasury. After having drawn the last dollar of specie out of the latter they could, by presenting an additional note, compel it to suspend again. Then gold would go up once more, perhaps to the full extent of the figure from which it would have fallen, and the clique could sell their specie in the market and realize their profit.

This is not only a possible occurrence; it is a probable one; a highly probable one; almost a certainty. There is nothing in the world to prevent it, except two things: First, the inability of a clique to raise $100,000,000; second, the possibility that the Treasury, in offering to redeem its issues, may, arbitrarily and unexpectedly, prefer notes of particular numbers or dates of issue. But these objections are frivolous. Experience has demonstrated that there is no difficulty whatever on the part of stock-jobbing cliques to raise $100,000,000, whilst, with regard to making preferred credits of certain notes, the Treasury has no authority to do so, and if it had, the exercise of such authority would be almost certain to be defeated through treachery. Secrets so weighty as this one would be, are impossible to keep. Even if it did not leak out, the clique would be certain to monopolize the Treasury doors to the exclusion of all comers. In short, wealth, power, organization, experience, and special training, would be ranged on the one side, against a scattered and indifferent population on the other; and who can doubt which would win?

Finally, even if carried out successfully, the exercise of such authority would be unlawful and unjust.

We cannot resume with $100,000,000, nor with $200,000,000. Why, gentlemen, we have had $140,000,000 in specie in the Treasury on several occasions during the past ten years. If it is practicable to resume now with $100,000,000, why was it not practicable on those occasions with $140,000,000? It was certainly not for lack of desire on the part of the Secretary of the Treasury, but simply because both the Secretary and Congress plainly saw that the thing could not be done.

It is better to be on the safe side of an operation of this magnitude and importance. It is better to have a dollar more than is necessary for the purpose of resuming, than a dollar less than is necessary. We cannot expect to resume upon false pretences. We cannot, and if we can, we ought not, hoodwink the people, or run the risk of failing, and, therefore, of unsettling values for an indefinite period in the future. In order to resume we must pay dollar for "dollar," and dollar for dollar, as the law now stands, means at least $350,000,000 in gold.

And now for the third time I ask, where are these $350,000,000 to come from? Gentlemen may differ with me as to the sum needed for resumption. Some may believe $200,000,000 are enough, others may even consider $100,000,000. I have briefly discussed these opinions, and do not believe that less than $350,000,000 will suffice. With only $129,500,000 of Bank of England and $144,000,000 of Provincial bank-notes afloat in 1815, total $273,500,000 in paper, England required over $270,000,000 in coin before she was enabled to resume. After you shall have resumed, less coin may be required in the country; but in order to resume, you will require a dollar in coin for every dollar of Government paper afloat, and. in my opinion, and, as shown by the experience of England, you will also have to give the national banks time to acquire an equal fund of specie, before they can resume; otherwise, you may bankrupt every one of them.

Confining myself to the strict requirement of the Government, I again ask where is the requisite specie to come from if we are to depend upon gold alone?

The annual gold product of the world is given at $97,500,000, of which let us say the whole amount can be retained in the Occident, which all will admit is a violent stretch of probability. It is estimated that considerably more than one-half of this supply is needed for the arts, for gilding, plating, watchcase making, jewelry, and the like.* Let us limit this demand to one-half: this would leave a supply of, say $49,000,000 of gold per annum, available for the maintenance and increase of money. The maintenance of money costs about one and a half per cent. per annum in abrasion and loss. One and a half per cent. on the present Occidental stock of $2,600,000,000 gold amounts to $39,000,000. This is the quantity of gold needed every year to maintain the existing stock of gold coin in the Occident. Deduct this from $49,000,000, the total annual supply available for money, and there would remain a surplus of $10,000,000 a year. It is out of this surplus that our $350,000,000 must come, unless it comes out of the existing stock in other countries, a point which will be considered farther on.

Upon the most favorable hypotheses, after according every debatable point in favor of the feasibility of the proposition, we should have to wait nearly thirty-five years to accomplish it in practice; for if we managed to obtain every

---

*Seyd.

ounce of gold which can be spared from the supplies of the world for the next thirty-five years we shall barely have secured enough.

There are considerations, however, which render some of these hypotheses untenable.

The entire population of the Occidental world is increasing at the rate of one per cent. per annum.* Even if its exchanges or their bases increased no faster than its population, this fact would require an annual addition of 1 per cent. to the stock of coin. At the present time this would absorb nearly $3,000,000 per annum.

The demand for gold in the arts will undoubtedly increase at, at least, an equal rate. The probability is that it will increase, because it has increased, at a greater ratio. Limiting it to this ratio, it will amount to nearly another $3,000,000 per annum.

The annual product of gold throughout the world is diminishing. It was $182,000,000 in 1852; it is given at only $97,500,000 in 1875. This is a decrement of over $3,500,000 per annum.

On account of these considerations we must subtract about $9,500,000 per annum from the world's available annual surplus of $10,000,000, leaving but $500,000 per annum to spare. At the rate of $500,000 per annum we shall need seven hundred years in which to garner up $350,000,000, the amount necessary wherewith to resume payment in gold!

The possibility of performing even this feat rests upon the assumption that Austria, which has a forced paper currency; and Italy, which has a forced paper currency; and Russia, which has a forced paper currency; and several other countries which have forced paper currencies; countries which in the aggregate contain one-half of the entire European population of the globe; will be content to wait until the United States gets its quantum of gold wherewith to resume, before they will make any move to effect a

* Essay on Population of the Earth in New York *Independent*.

similar reform in their own currencies. It rests, also, upon the assumption that the people of the United States will wait during these years for the consummation of resumption: wait without complaint, without further legislation, without getting tired, or yielding to the clamors of interest, or prejudice, or ignorance.

RESUMPTION ON A GOLD BASIS IMPOSSIBLE.

I tell you, gentlemen, the thing cannot be done! Resumption in gold is out of the question. It is not practical financially, it is not practical metallurgically, it is not practical internationally, it is not practical politically, in short it is not practical at all.

I can no longer wonder that the Interchangeable Theory or any other form of paper lunacy has obtained a footing in the land. So long as intelligent and educated men will persist in attempting to do that which the most unintelligent and uneducated plainly perceive to be impossible, so long will demagoguery and roguery have a footing! "My plan," they will say "is at least as good as theirs;" meaning that of the gold resumptionists. And I must confess that I assent to their proposition. One plan is quite as good as the other, and not a whit better. They are both utterly impracticable, and no attempt to carry out either one of them can have any other than one ending: failure, violent fluctuations and unsettlement of values, distress, commotion, and the grave dangers that lurk beneath all violent upheavals of the body politic.

There are two forms of reply that I anticipate to the assertion that it is impossible in less than a great number of years to obtain the requisite supply of metal wherewith to resume specie payments in gold. One is, if money is merely a measure of values, why will not $100,000,000 or even $50,000,000 measure values as well as $350,000,000 or any other sum? The puerility involved in this reply needs little further response than what has already been accorded to it in a previous portion of this speech. If there was no accumulated stock of coin in the world, upon which values throughout the world already rested; if there were existing no contracts, rents, leases, bonds, mortgages, and the like, executed in the past and maturing now, or executed now and to mature in the future; in a word, if the world was born to-day, $50,000,000 would in theory answer quite as well for the entire money of this country, aye, even of the whole world, as any other sum. But the world was not born to-day, nor yesterday, nor the day before. The stock of coin which forms the substratum of the world's prices is the accumulation of fifty centuries, and bargains are being made every day—for example, Government and corporative debts—which cover long periods of time. To disturb these prices and contracts by forcing the exchanges of the country to be measured by a sum of specie so vastly less than its usual measure, as $100,000,000 or even $200,000,000 would be, would be tantamount to the violent destruction of vast interests and a wrenching of all the relations of industrial and social life. Imagine workingmen's wages at twelve-and-a-half cents a day in this country, while they stood at $2 in France or England. Imagine our railway corporations forced to pay their rents on long leases, and the interest on long bonds, in daily appreciating gold. Would not this be quite as unjust as, on the other hand, by issuing a daily depreciating interchangeable token, to gratuitously save them from that disaster?

The other reply that I anticipate to the objection that we cannot obtain gold enough wherewith to resume, is this: "We can obtain the gold from Europe." Can we? Let us examine this point.

CAN WE GET GOLD ENOUGH FROM EUROPE WHEREWITH TO RESUME SPECIE PAYMENTS?

When a merchant purposes to buy a large quantity of a given article, his first thought is to compute how much his demand will raise the price of the article during the progress of the purchase. The first element in this calculation is the stock on hand, the next is the current supply and demand. It is the same with the stock operator, in short, with dealers in all commodities. Why should it not be the same with Government when it goes into the market for $350,000,000 of gold ?

The current demand and supply of this article has been discussed. There is no stock of it on hand in the same sense that there is a stock or accumulation of merchandise. The stock of merchandise is the unused portion—the surplus. There is no unused stock of gold coin in the world, no surplus. It is all in use to support prices; * withdraw it, and the whole fabric of prices and credits falls to the dust. The stock of gold in Europe and the countries settled by Europeans amounts to about $2,600,000,000. On every one of these dollars stands a vast and almost toppling superstructure of credits in every conceivable form. You now propose to purchase one-eighth, almost one-seventh, of this entire basis of the rest of the Occidental world's exchanges and credits. Do you believe you can do it? Do you believe you can offer your bonds or your merchandise in the markets of Europe low enough to purchase with them $350,000,000 of gold? Do you suppose that United States 5 per cent. bonds at par, or 90, or 80, or even 70, will accomplish it? Or, to put it another way, suppose you determine not to sell your bonds under par: do you suppose that you can place them at any rate of interest to which the self-respect of this country would submit, or which its resources would justify? Do you suppose that when you commenced to draw gold from Europe, the Bank of England and other like institutions, would not raise their rate of interest to 7, 8, 10, or even 12 per cent.? You know that this is always done when specie is observed to be flowing out. You know that it must be done. And do you suppose that when it is done that you can place your bonds at any lower rate of interest than the bank rate? Do you imagine that American produce or manufactures offered to Europe at three-fourths of their present market prices will do it ?

* The legal tender portion at a full ratio of activity; the subsidiary coins at a lesser rate.

Well, then, I do not. To induce Europe and the European world to part with one-seventh of its measure of exchanges and basis of credit, within the time fixed for the resumption of specie payment in this country, you would have to sell all your moveables—for remember that lands, which constitute more than one-half of our wealth, cannot be exported—at prices which would bankrupt every industry in this country. You might get $10,000,000, or $20,000,000, or, perhaps, even $50,000,000, in gold. By dint of hammering the bond market (and you would have to authorize the Treasury to sell below par, at any price the bonds would fetch) during the two years and a half now remaining, you might even get $100,000,000 of metal; but when you shall have taken $100,000,000 away from Europe you will have produced a commotion and a fall in prices on the other side, that, if it did not lead to the closure of the European stock markets to American bonds, would certainly precipitate a tremendous financial convulsion.* As for this side, the effects would be no less alarming.

Recollect, gentlemen, that the problem is that of taking $350,000,000 in gold out of a fully occupied and heavily over-topped basis of only $2,600,000,000 in the Occidental world. It is not the whole stock of metal, both silver and gold, that we can now call upon, as in former days. Silver has been demonetized in several countries of Europe; it has been demonetized here. We have thoughtlessly so

---

* "When the negotiations were going on in London for the sale of the largest amount of United States bonds that have ever been sold there at one time, it was foreseen by the Bank of England that a quantity of coin would accumulate as the proceeds of these bonds to the credit of the Government of the United States. As a matter of fact there was an accumulation of about $21,000,000. The Bank of England, foreseeing that there would be an accumulation of coin to the credit of the United States, which might be taken away bodily in specie, gave notice to the officers of the Treasury Department of the United States that the power of that institution would be arrayed against the whole proceeding unless we gave a pledge that the coin should not be removed, and that we would reinvest it in the bonds of the United States as they were offered in the markets of London. *We were compelled to comply!*"—*Speech of Senator Boutwell, formerly Secretary of the Treasury.* (*Cong. Record*, 43*d Cong.*, 1*st Session, vol.* 2, *part* 6, *p.* 23 *of Appendix.*)

worded our laws that, until we alter them, we can only pay in gold. The Latin Union, Germany and Scandinavia, together with England and Portugal, &c., have so worded their laws, whether thoughtlessly or not, you can decide for yourselves, that gold alone is the legal-tender in those countries for the payment of large sums, and its value is the standard of all payments, large or small. We would demand of them one-seventh of their entire stock, which now, unlike the period from 1848 to 1865, is not increasing; which, in fact, has a strong tendency to decrease. Who, under these circumstances, will have the hardihood to assert that this problem is a practical one? And who will venture to deny that, if it is solved at all, it can only be solved at a sacrifice more overwhelming than any which has presented itself to the consideration of financiers since the study of money, its functions and its vicissitudes, first became a science?

OUR INTEREST CHARGE ANOTHER OBSTACLE TO RESUMPTION IN GOLD.

On top of the many insuperable difficulties which lie in the way of resumption in gold, lies another one which is as great as any of them, and which you would augment by attempting to resume in gold. I allude to the interest on the public debt, which debt is very largely held abroad. This interest now amounts to nearly $100,000,000 per annum. By selling bonds to the extent of $350,000,000, say at 10 per cent.—for it is perhaps hopeless to expect to do it at a lesser sacrifice—you will add $35,000,000 a year to your gold interest debt, and those $35,000,000 to the portion held abroad. Where are these $35,000,000 to come from? Where are the whole $135,000,000 to come from? Your annual interest charge will alone amount to more than the whole world's product of gold. So far as the portion of it which is paid to bondholders in this country is concerned, it may stay here and be thrown upon the market, and purchased by the Government, and so used over and over again, as is the case now. But not so with the portion that goes abroad. You cannot hope to get any of that back without selling the merchandise of the country at lower rates than Europeans will be willing to take for similar merchandise of their own production, and after you shall have drained Europe of one-fifth of its specie, (one-seventh of the whole Occidental world's, or one-fifth of Europe's,) prices will fall to a very low point there, and you would have to sell very low to compete. Are your farmers ready to deliver their wheat in Europe at the rate of 40 or 50 cents a bushel? Are your manufacturers prepared to sell their cotton prints at 2 cents a yard?

I warn you, gentlemen, that the attempt will be futile; that the thought is absurd; that the whole theory of endeavoring to destroy one-half of the world's accumulation of the precious metals or of taking part in the attempt, as you would do by attempting to resume in gold alone, is sheer madness.

COMPARATIVE EASE OF RESUMING IN THE DOUBLE STANDARD.

Now let us contrast with this impracticable scheme the ease of resuming specie payments in both the metals, or, on the basis of that double standard which the world has used for thirty centuries, and after an endless variety of experiments, without being able to dispense with it or even venturing to trifle with it until Change Alley found that money was to be gained by inducing these experiments to be made in England and on the Continent.

If we resolve to resume in gold and silver, instead of having to draw upon a fund of $2,600,000,000 and an annual supply of $97,500,000, as in the case of gold alone, we would have a fund of $5,700,000,000 and an annual supply of $170,000,000 to draw upon. Not only is the fund more than twice as great, and the supply nearly twice as great, but both the fund and the supply are more widely distributed. Instead of having to draw upon the Occident alone, we would have the whole World to draw upon. Three hundred and fifty millions in gold form one-seventh of the entire stock of that metal; the same sum in both the metals forms less than one-sixteenth of the entire stock. If a draft of one-seventh would occasion a fall in prices of 15 per cent., a draft of less than one-sixteenth would occasion a decline of less than 6 per cent.; and while 15 per cent., during two-and-a-half years—equal to 6 per cent per annum—would sweep away all and more than all the profits of industry, which, on the whole, do not net over 3 or 4 per cent., 6 per cent. in two-and-a-half years, equal to 2⅖ per cent. per annum, would enable us to get back to a sound measure of values without the loss of more than a very small portion of our current industrial profits.

It has been objected to the monetization of silver by the United States that the Comstock lode was vomiting forth a vast surplus of that metal. It is only to be regretted that this is not the fact; for if gentlemen will consult the statistics of the precious metals, they will perceive that since 1852, when the product of gold and silver was $223,000,000, the annual supply has fallen off so that in 1875 it was but $170,000,000, and in 1876 will probably not be more. There is therefore great danger of a dearth of metal, and it would be fortunate if the yield of the Comstock lode were more prolific than it is.

My fear is that this prolificity, such as it is, will have reached its maximum within the present year. It is the candid opinion of a man who has devoted nearly thirty years of his life to the practical working and management of gold and silver mines that, so far the Comstock lode is concerned, and he is entirely familiar with this great silver deposit, we have arrived at the beginning of the end. We now know the probable dimensions and bearings of the ore producing chimneys, and can very plainly foresee their early exhaustion. Whatever the fact may be with regard to the Comstock lode, and at best it is but matter of opinion, we know that for the present and so far as we can see ahead, the combined annual product of the two metals throughout the world, as compared with late years, is decreasing.

If now the question be asked: Where will you get your $350,000,000 from, upon which to resume? the best answer we can make is: From the world at large; from a stock of $5,700,000,000 in gold and silver coin; from an annual supply of $170,000,000; from Europe, from Mexico and South America, from Asia, and, readiest and best of all, from our own mines.

In buying metal from the rest of the world, as we should have to do had we no great mines of our own, we should have to buy it with the accumulated charges of transport and coinage upon it. In buying it from our own mines we can buy it at its worth upon the spot of production, without transportation or coinage, or interest charges upon it.

RESTORATION OF THE DOUBLE STANDARD AND OUR MINING INTERESTS.

And here let me say that the mining interests of this country are represented not, as some persons absurdly suppose, by a few millionaires, but for the most part by a vast number of persons, with no other resources than their intelligent minds and willing hands, who work in the mines for daily bread, and by a scarcely less numerous class of small proprietors, themselves also workingmen, who hold each a few shares in the mines in which they are employed.

The miners of the West are among the most stalwart and spirited yeoman in the world. They are inured to danger and toil, and are brave, strong, intelligent, and self-reliant. In weary processions across alkaline deserts, under equatorial and blistering suns, across mountain and valley, desert and plain, amidst the attacks of savages and the fevers of tropical swamps, they marked the path and blazed the trail of Western Empire. They overcame every hostile condition and builded, on foundations of Liberty and Justice, three great States in your western border. They conquered the Genius of Sterility in its stronghold, built cities 10,000 feet above the level of the sea and hewed out thrifty workshops 2,500 feet below the surface of the earth. They have organized mining with the exactness and thoroughness of science, and in this respect placed this country in the vanguard of the nations. They have neither avoided your tax-gatherers, sought your subsidies, nor demanded your protective legislation. Nor do they do so now. They only ask that you shall legislate in respect of this great question in view of the history of the world, the Constitution of the country, and the facts that surround you.

While the miners of this country have the highest right both by reason of their birth, their indomitable love of freedom, and the perilous nature of their industry, to demand both favor and advantage from the Government, they do not ask for either. But they demand that the Constitution shall be respected, and the laws enforced under which they established the great industry which they represent. They know full well that the world's accumulated stock of silver is too vast and the annual diminution from abrasion and loss too great, to fear any permanent or continued fall in the price of that metal. They know that silver must continue to remain the money of a main part of the world for centuries to come, and that it cannot be dispensed with in any part of the world. They understand too well the fluctuating character of the supplies of gold, to fear that this metal will permanently usurp the place of silver in the money of the world, or in the money of any considerable part of the world. They perfectly well comprehend the fact that the present slight fall of silver is due to the mad attempt to demonetize it wholly or partly in the countries of the Latin Union and Germany, and are not at all alarmed, either as to the success of this attempt or the future price of silver. They believe, as Jefferson said in discussing this very same subject nearly a century ago, that the world's long and constantly-tried experience of silver is a kind of precedent which it is tolerably safe to trust to.

Our miners understand that silver is of constant, steady, and moderate supply; keeping pace with the world's expanding industry, and no more. They understand that gold is of inconstant, fluctuating, and either superabundant or inadequate supply; and they have no fears as to the marketability of their silver product.

The question before us is therefore not one of favor or advantage to any industry, even though that industry be largely American and of a nature and importance that should command for it every advantage which legislation could confer.

RESTORATION OF THE DOUBLE STANDARD A NATIONAL AFFAIR.

The question is one of advantage to the nation, to society, to the world at large. It has to deal not only with the industrial interests of to-day, but of all time. It is the question of the measure which shall be applied not only to the labor of the present time, but to the labor of all time past, the labor of all time to come. It proposes to guage this labor by the measure which has guaged it forever—by the guage that can measure it most fairly and equitably; by the only guage that can truly measure it at all—to wit, the double standard of gold and silver. It is opposed to the impracticable project of measuring it by a new and smaller measure; by an inconstant, a fluctuating, a monopolized measure. This is the nature and magnitude of the question before us; a question to the elucidation of which the most intellectual men of all nations and in all times have largely devoted their attention; a question which lies down at the very basis of property, of industry and of progress; a question which not only affects the wealth of nations, the rank of nations, the welfare of nations, but the very conditions of social existence itself.

It is too large, it is too grand a question to be belittled by any such vulgar and familiar approaches as have, I regret to say, been made toward it by one or two gentlemen who have alluded to the subject in the House of Representatives. Fifty centuries of the world's accumulated wealth are before us to be answered in our deliberations upon this question; fifty centuries of mute, but colossal interrogatories; fifty centuries of trial, of suffering, of toil, of conflict, of ever perishing and ever renewing human life, every element of which has contributed, one way or another, to mould the ponderous scale of the precious metals in which the work of the world is measured, and which some madmen would raise their Vandal hands to destroy.

These men are chiefly the plutocrats of England and

Germany. They want the debts which the nations of the earth owe to them, and which were made in Manchester cottons and Birmingham wares, to be paid, not in the base currencies in which they were nominally or really engendered—not even in good money, in gold and silver, which is the money of the world, and has been so for all time—but in that particular metal which they have observed is for the time diminishing in supply and daily becoming more difficult and expensive to purchase. To accomplish this object they are ready to revolutionize the currency of the world; to help demonetize, and advise others to help demonetize, a stock of over $2,000,000,000 of silver, the precious moiety of the world's standard of values, stored up from the ages, and in its place to set up their own mooncalf of gold, recking not how much suffering the inadequate substitution will occasion.

LET ENGLAND AND GERMANY ADHERE TO THE GOLD STANDARD IF THEY WILL.

The worst punishment which can befall this reckless trifling with the interests of society, is that which it itself invites, and which must befall it if the rest of the world refuses to take part in such trifling. By leaving England and Germany to the enjoyment of their self-erected standard of gold, it would result in the end that gold would become cheaper in those countries than elsewhere and prices would rise therein. The co-ordinate use of silver with gold in the rest of the world would tend to drive gold into England and Germany, where it would accumulate and become cheap. Gold would inevitably flow into the countries where it was most in demand, viz: England and Germany, just as now silver flows into Asia. And as silver has accumulated in Asia and enhanced the prices of commodities and services in that portion of the world, so would gold accumulate in England and Germany and enhance the prices of commodities and services there. When this happened, and the plutocrat perceived that his fund or his income of gold would purchase less of other men's labor than before, his punishment will have arrived, and richly will he have deserved it.

What will then be his resource, his only resource from the loss of purchasing power? The same resource to which his narrow selfishness has always instinctively led him: that of endeavoring to change the standard to the dearer metal, which will then be silver. He will then have to purchase his silver from us, as he now asks that we shall purchase his gold from him, and we shall be able to fix as high a price upon silver as he would now fix upon gold.

TO ADHERE TO THE GOLD STANDARD IN THE UNITED STATES IS TO GRATUITOUSLY ENHANCE THE MORTGAGES UPON THE NATION.

The true meaning of the sinister advice which we receive from this class, is, that, by adopting the gold standard, we should gratuitously and needlessly enhance the value of the mortgages, which, in the shape of Government bonds, they hold upon the industries of this country. We are not ashamed of these mortgages. Though they were given for inadequate consideration, yet they were given in a time of peril and uncertainty. We have not the slightest intention to repudiate them. We have already paid upon them in interest vastly more than their entire face, and shall continue to pay this interest promptly and as fast as it comes due. But while it is neither to our taste, (for we are a proud nation, and disdain to submit our honor to the scant measure of a doubtful law) nor to our interest, to repudiate our obligations, we do not propose to go beyond the limit which our organic laws have set to the standard in which debts shall be paid. We do not propose, by resuming specie payments in gold, to increase the demand for and purchasing power of gold, and thus enhance the value of the mortgages upon our industry. The law of this country made our standard the bi-metallic one of gold and silver. This is not only the law of the United States; it is the law of nations; the law of ages; the law of the World. We refuse to be led up and down hill, first into one standard and then into the other, at the beck of a short-sighted and selfish class of men, to whom the world owes no debt of gratitude. We refuse to pull up and destroy our ancient moorings. We refuse to part with the ages and with the rest of the world, to which both our present and our future interests unite us; to the rest of Europe; to South America, to Africa, and to Asia. We propose to stand where we have always stood; where the nations stand; where stands the world; we propose to stand on the double standard; the standard of the populations; the standard which the natural fitness and general distribution of the precious metals has indicated to be the only safe one.

GOLD AND SILVER MINING UNPROFITABLE, AND TO INTERRUPT IS TO DESTROY IT.

There is great danger, I might even without exaggeration say, appalling danger, in abandoning the double standard. This arises from the fact that the mining of the precious metals is, on the average, always conducted upon the verge of loss. Therefore the moment you demonetize one metal you temporarily cheapen it, and help to throw it out of production. To stop production is the work of an instant, to reinstate it again is the work of years; and when, as is bound to be the case, the discarded metal is once more in demand, it is the work of long time to obtain sufficient supplies of it again. We know that in the case of the Siberian gold mines over three thousand years elapsed between the time of their abandonment (by the Persians) and reoccupation (by the Russians); in the case of the Spanish silver mines fifteen hundred years; in the case of the Mexican silver mines, during the first half of this century, some twenty or thirty years. It matters not what the cause of these several abandonments was; whether it was wars, or the insufficiency of known mechanical resources, or trifling with the standard. It is sufficient if we know that no matter what cause put an end to the production of the metals, the most urgent after demand for the abandoned metal was inadequate for a long period to stimulate its reproduction.

When mines are abandoned, water flows into them and fills them up; earth, stones, and other debris clog and choke them, and frequently bury them up out of sight and even remembrance; the supporting timbers of galleries rot away, the galleries themselves fall in; and these circumstances often render it practically impossible to reopen the mines. And you cannot find silver and gold mines at pleasure, as you can wheat fields or suitable sites for mills or manufactories. The whole surface of Central America and California, and the Sierra Nevadas has been ripped and torn up in the search for the precious metals. The valleys have been explored, the streams turned from their natural courses, the hills washed away with artificial hydraulic power, the mountains honey-combed with shafts and tunnels. Not a district has been left undisturbed. The Pacific coast of America has been ransacked in modern days even more thoroughly than were Northern Africa and the Spanish Peninsula in ancient days; for this ransacking has been done by the hardiest among the foremost races of the world.

But in the exploration of natural resources man has no pity for Nature or posterity. He exploits the land in the pursuit of agriculture as our Virginian forefathers did the noble valleys of the Atlantic coast in the cultivation of tobacco; as the planters of the cotton States did the table lands of Georgia and Alabama and the bottom lands of Mississippi in the cultivation of cotton; as the western men are now doing the richly-wooded lands of their country, for the sake of the timber which stands upon them. In a similar way have the Pacific States been exploited for mines.

There are probably but few, of even measuredly, rich deposits left to discover. The most that we can henceforth do is to exhaust what have been found. There are no more great bonanzas in the the Sierra Nevadas; probably there are not elsewhere in the world deposits of ore of such magnitude. I do not mean deposits found; I mean found or unfound.*

Already many of the less profitable silver mines of the world have ceased to be worked. The slight and temporary fall in silver, occasioned by the partial demonetization of the metal in Europe, its prospective practical demonetization in this country, and the hitherto abundant yield of the bonanza mines, have been sufficient to throw many of the poorer paying silver mines of the world out of production.†

By resuming specie payments in this country upon the basis of the fatally erroneous law of 1873 we would render practical and immediate that demonetization of silver which, as yet, while paper notes form nearly the entire circulating media of the country, is but prospective, and therefore not practical. More than this: the example of so great a country as the United States would be apt to lead other countries into the same erroneous way, and silver would soon become entirely demonetized in the Occidental world.

---

*It must always be borne in mind that the order of progress in mining is from the poor to the richer, just as the venerable and celebrated Henry C. Carey has shown it to be in agriculture. This order of progress in mining results from the fact that men always seek first the most easily accessible sources of production. When the outcroppings of a great mine are discovered it is rare that exploration proceeds further than a few hundred feet beneath the surface where the ore lies in widespread lenticular masses. Then comes the "barren zone," which is seldom explored at first. The richer but fewer deposits of ore below, the great bonanzas, concentrate in perpendicular veins far apart, and are never reached except at great outlay and expense, and as the result of organized and scientific mining. Whoever is fortunate enough to strike one of these bonanzas makes great profit from it, whilst the others sustain loss, and on the whole the product of metal is diminished.

†This fact is not only deducible from the statistics of the World's annual yield of silver given above, but it has come under my own observation that many of the low grade ore deposits, even of the Comstock lode, have either been abandoned or soon will be abandoned. These low grade mines, though fully provided with shafts, adits, railways, engines, mills, etc., which were profitably employed while silver bore a higher price in market, are being abandoned, the improvements put upon them are lost, and great numbers of miners have been thrown out of employment.

Did gold promise to continue in very abundant supply the ruinous consequences of this error might to some extent be mitigated; though under no circumstances could they be entirely mitigated, owing to the always fluctuating nature of gold supplies. But even this degree of mitigation is not to be expected. Gold is so far from being produced throughout the world in great abundance, that the present annual product is dangerously insufficient, and even this supply is declining. We are invited to abandon a good ship and enter a sinking one; to desert solid ground and stand upon a quagmire; to renounce a system which has stood the test of centuries, and adopt one which has been tried but by a single nation, England, and that only since 1816, or rather from 1824 to 1848, and at the expense of retarding and crushing the prosperity of her industrial classes during the period of such trial.

I have said that the mining of the precious metals is always conducted, on the average, upon the verge of loss. This statement is supported by all writers upon the subject.

The ready marketability of the precious metals, a fact which renders the product of the miner's labor available on the instant, forms a strong inducement to their production, and the competition is so great as to push the production to the verge of loss, perhaps even beyond it. The moment you destroy or impair this marketability of the precious metals, as you do by demonetizing silver, you diminish the production. You could not do the same with wheat or other commodities. Upon these the laws confer no privilege of marketability; they are not legal tender for the payment of debts. Their production, therefore, never ventures beyond the area of profit—I mean, of course, profit on the average. Present and future demand alone regulate their supply. It is not the same with the precious metals. Their supply has reference to the past as well as the present and future. There is a stock of these metals in the world which has come down to us from the earliest ages of history, and every additional ounce produced, affects this stock. There is no similar stock of any other commodities. Even arable lands and stone edifices fail to escape the ravages of time. With metal produced to-day you can discharge obligations for commodities and services sold or rendered years ago. You cannot do the same with wheat or any other commodities. Why? Because the laws make the precious metals legal tenders for the payment of debt. You cannot force a creditor to receive payment in wheat or lands, but you can force him to accept payment in money. Hence the superior marketability of the precious metals—a marketability which is due, in the first place, to their intrinsic qualities of superior homogeneity, divisibility, re-unitability, portability, etc., and in the second place to the law.

If you impair this marketability by demonetizing one of the metals, you reduce it to the same rank as any other commodity, to the rank of commodities which are produced only when such production is profitable. You will not destroy the production of the demonetized metal. Far from it. The precious metals are too valuable for a great variety of industrial purposes. They will still continue to be produced, only the quantity produced will be less; and after the stock of demonetized coin shall be absorbed irretrievably into the arts, the price will be higher. Why? Because the production of the metal will only be continued where it proves profitable. The supply will become regulated by the present and future demand. Rather than push the production of the metal to the verge of loss, men will prefer to engage in some other occupation. The price will not only rise on account of diminished production, but also, and chiefly, because the producer will demand in it a profit. Now he does not; he cannot. The competition is too keen to admit of profit. The production of the precious metals is perhaps, even on the whole, a constant source of loss. Still men will engage in it, not only on account of the occasional fortunate and unexpected prizes which it yields, and which is the same in diamond washing and pearl fishing, but also because of the superior, the instant, marketability of the product. This instant marketability is due in part to the law. It enables the gold or silver miner to realize the product of his labor at once. It induces him to make the most of that labor; it leads him to overwork; and eventually it destroys him. The valleys of El Dorado are strewn with the wrecks of human lives, wrecks which lie bleaching in the sun to warn away the newcomer. But they warn in vain; and the production of the precious metals continues in spite of loss, and sickness, and premature death. Conducted at this great sacrifice, conducted thus always upon the verge of loss, and perhaps beyond it, the moment the production of the precious metals, or either of them, is discouraged by demonetization, from that moment it sinks to the rank of all other commodities and demands a profit in its price. Suppose you demonetize silver, and thus limit its production to the extent of the demand for it in the arts; and when the stock of silver coin becomes melted up and absorbed, as it soon would be, you discover, as you will be sure to discover, that you have made a mistake: at what price is it imagined can this silver be repurchased? At 15 for 1 of gold? At 12 for 1, 10 for 1, 8, for 1? I fancy not. Gold was demonetized in Japan, and not more than twenty-five years ago it could be purchased in that country at four times the price of silver. Later on they re-monetized gold in that country, and were obliged to purchase it at the rate of 1 for 15½ of silver.

Had Japan not been a country at that period very backward in civilization, divided into great feudatories, whose tributes and rents were payable in grain, the difficulty of again monetizing the discarded metal would have been insuperable. Even as it was, the measure was accompanied by a violent social revolution and the entire destruction of the existing system of government.

Are you prepared to hazard an experiment of this character? For the sake of pursuing the idle, mischievous theory called monometalism, urged by an interested, selfish, and shortsighted class of men in England and Germany, and indorsed by certain flippant and conceited writers on political economy, are you ready to invoke the tremendous risk of banishing a metal which constitutes one-half of the world's stock of money, and which, if once banished, can never be recalled without the propitiating sacrifice of all vested interests, of all existing relations of property, of all the institutions of society? The great institution of Japan was the feudal system, and the moment she opened herself to the influence upon prices and relations which was exercised by the precious metal which she had previously forbidden to compose part of her standard, that great institution was shivered to atoms. The great institution of the United States is popular suffrage. Are we prepared, by abandoning the olden way, the double standard, and exposing ourselves to the social revolution which, after abandoning that standard, would inevitably accompany its re-establishment—are we prepared to see *our* great institution shivered to atoms, too?

It cannot be doubted that resumption in specie and limitation to the single gold standard would, in time, produce these alarming results. But we are not a people who would open the door to such consequences. We would endeavor to obviate them. And the only way to obviate them would be to go on with irredeemable paper, with violent abberrations of prices, with bankruptcies, and with the pandemonium of the stock exchange.

THE DOUBLE STANDARD WILL HAVE TO BE RESTORED.

There are, perhaps, those who do not perceive any reason which would compel a nation to return to the double standard after having abandoned it. These reasons have already been given, and I regard them as unanswerable. They are:

1. The insufficient stock of gold in the world to effect its exchanges without a great, rapid, and overwhelming fall in prices to one-half of present prices in specie.

2. The insufficient annual supplies of gold; there not being more than enough produced to supply the arts and maintain the stock of coin.

3. The fluctuating nature of gold production, which would give rise to violent aberrations of prices from time to time.

4. The monopolization of the supply of gold, which now is chiefly from countries covered by the British flag.

And many other reasons, which these few will serve, perhaps, to recall.

When the tremendous decline and violent fluctuations in prices which must accompany a single gold standard, have worked as much ruin and destruction of existing relations as the nation will bear, the revulsion in favor of again monetizing silver will be too great to resist; yet re-monetization may have to be effected in the face of difficulties and dangers quite as great as those from which escape is sought to be made. It would be Charybdis on one side; Scylla on the other; mischief, danger, ruin on both.

At the bottom of this dangerous effort to abolish the double standard of this country, lies nothing but selfishness and injustice—the selfishness of a class who desire to receive payment for debts and obligations in a metal which, for the moment, and at the mean natural relation is a few per cent. dearer than the other.

SOCIETY CAN ONLY BE RULED WITH EQUITY—THE GOLD STANDARD INEQUITABLE.

Opposed to the consummation of this injustice, not only does all Nature array herself, but so also do the unconscious instincts of humanity, the occult working of social institutions. Consummate it, if you can, and you will have poverty, distress, commotion, and perhaps revolution. Having consummated it, try, then, to undo it, and you will find the task beset with great difficulties.

Neglected dislocations of the human frame are difficult to remedy; because the wrenched member finds for itself a new socket. The dislocation of the social fabric which threatens to result from the effects of the act of 1873 may yet be averted by the timely measure of restoring the double standard before we attempt to resume specie payments.

You cannot expect to take a nation by the throat, hold it down, squeeze the last drop of substance out of it, no matter in what sacred name, whether of Honor or Justice, without running the risk of being taken by the throat yourselves. No matter how cunning the injustice is, it is sure to be found out when it comes to work, and sure to be avenged when it is found out. All the interests of society, even the safety and permanence of vested interests, demand the exercise of equity in the affairs of government; and I tell those who represent such interests that, in the long run, they will best consult their advantage in being just at the outset. They have got the people of this country by the throat in the ambiguously worded act of February 25, 1862. They pinned the people down by the coin-paying act of March 18, 1869, and now they would squeeze the last drop of substance out of them by the single gold standard act of February, 1873, which they propose to carry into effect by the Resumption Act (a very proper act of itself) of 1875. And now my advice to them is, to stop and undo the worst part of their work, by repealing so much of the act of 1873 as prevents the silver dollar from being tendered for the payment of debts. The people have paid their full ransom to Brennus; let him not attempt to overload the scale with the weight of his sword, or they may take it up and use it.

OUR COMMERCE WITH ASIA DEPENDS UPON THE DOUBLE STANDARD.

Turning from these considerations of danger in abolishing the double standard to those of profit and advantage in retaining it, permit me to call your attention to the influence which this subject is destined to exercise upon our commerce.

It has been the interest in all ages of certain classes to deny that Commerce is beneficial, and that agriculture and manufactures or mining are alone entitled to political consideration; but such a position is utterly untenable. Production cannot advance beyond the rudest limits without commerce, whose essential function it is to exchange that which is not needed, for that which is, or, to remove commodities from places where they are not wanted, to places where they are. In fact, commerce is inseparably bound up with production; there is no actual dividing line between them. The carriage of seeds to be planted, of textiles to be woven, of ores to be smelted, and the removal of the results to places of deposit or consumption, are all commercial functions. Foreign commerce is in like manner inseparable from production, and forms part of it. The implements, materials, agencies, and even remoter sources of national productive industries, depend upon foreign commerce, and would perish without it. Commerce has exercised a potent influence in propagating and extending religion. In its train have ever followed opulence, national strength, political liberty, letters, arts, and sciences. Its advance has always been marked by a general progress in the condition of men; its retardation by a corresponding retrogradation; and its discouragement or decline by poverty, national dissolution, tyranny, slavery, ignorance, and crime. It has destroyed the barriers of distance, alienage, race, religion, and caste. It has equalized the conditions of life in various parts of the earth, and tended to promote that homogeneousness of the human race which the profoundest thinkers have maintained is an indispensable preliminary to its highest development.

Asia Major, with the products of its varied climes and its teeming populations of Tartary, Persia, India, China, and Japan, has in all ages been the objective point of commerce, and the nations who found the best route to it, have, in turn, all held the sceptre of commercial greatness. The Phœnicians opened a route (not the ancient canal of Necho) to Asia by way of Suez; the Hebrews, overland, by way of Palmyra or Tadmor. The Suez route was reopened by the Greeks and successively kept open by the Romans and Venetians. The Genoese penetrated to Asia by way of the Euxine; the Portugese led the way by the Cape of Good Hope; the Hansards opened an overland route by way of Novgorod; Spain sought for a path westward and stumbled upon a New World; England discovered a route by way of Cape Horn, and America has paved with iron rails, first one route by way of Panama and afterward another *via* San Francisco. France has acquired both glory and profit by reopening the long-abandoned Suez canal of the Egyptians; England has reawakened the commercial hopes of her statesmen by purchasing a large interest in this canal; the Medieval prosperity of Italy has been revived through her proximity to it; and Russia is exciting the jealousy of England by extending her borders and military posts to the northwestern limits of India.

The commercial diadem of the world, the commerce with Asia, lies within easier grasp of the United States than that of any other nation of the Occident. We not only possess the two shortest or best routes to the Orient, those by way of Panama and San Francisco; we are not only in fact the next-door neighbor to Japan and China, stretching, as our possessions do, within sight of Kamskatka and holding almost the entire shores of the northeastern Pacific; we are not only at peace with Asia, and regarded by her with more friendliness than any other nation—we possess that commercial object for which Asia is as anxious to seek the Occident as we are the Orient for tea, spices, and silk. We are at the present moment the largest producers of silver in the world, and silver is the main, almost the only, object of foreign commerce to Asiatics. Even yet, although Europe has for centuries been pouring what silver she could spare into Asia; although all of Atahualpa's treasures and almost all the silver product of Mexico has found its way to Asia Major, the price of agricultural labor in that country is scarcely more than a penny a day, and the taxes levied by its monarchs are paid in rice. These facts prove the necessity and demand for silver in Asia and the comparative scarcity of it even at the present day.

I have already stated that it is estimated that Asia possessed a stock of coin, almost entirely silver, amounting at the beginning of the present century to about $700,000,000; in 1829 to about $800,000,000; in 1848 to about $900,000,000; and in 1872 to about $2,100,000,000. With a population, stationary, and of, say, 700,000,000, this amounted to one dollar *per capita* at the beginning of the century and three dollars *per capita* at the present time.

Merely to keep this stock of coin preserved from the effects of abrasion and loss, Asia requires some $30,000,000 in silver every year. To increase it, she requires more.

Suppose we persist in demonetizing our silver, suppose we lessen the demand for its use in the Occident and help to throw upon the markets of the world a stock of silver which we must replace with a stock of gold: is it not patent to the humblest understanding that we would lower its value, and be obliged to sell it to Asia, who, having then no competitor for its possession, would be likely to obtain it at a very low price in her commodities? Is it not plain that under such circumstances, and for a long series of years to come, our annual product of silver would follow the way of our rejected stock, and fall into the hands of the Orient at a degraded price. Should we not have to pay more, much more, than now, for the teas, spices, silk, rice, textiles, and other raw materials which we obtain from that quarter of the world? And were we obliged, eventually, as I believe we should be, to buy back this thoughtlessly demonetized and abandoned stock of silver, should we not have to purchase it at a very high price, seeing that meanwhile all prices in Asia would have become greatly enhanced?

Hence if we let slip the present favorable opportunity to purchase silver for the purposes of resumption we may find it very difficult to do so in future. When Occidental silver once gets to the Orient it rarely returns and it never will return in any considerable quantity until the scale of prices in the two great divisions of the globe become more nearly equalized than they are at present. This may be centuries hence.

Nature has furnished us with such advantages for seeking the commerce of Asia, advantages of route, of amicable relations, of an ample supply of silver, that if we do not senselessly throw them away, we are almost certain to monopolize the Asiatic trade and the vast profits that accrue from its pursuit. Asia stands in urgent need of silver; that silver we possess, and she must now come to us for it and purchase it from us, and, as we can afford to sell it to her cheaper than Europe can, by the difference of carriage, insurance, interest, commissions, &c., we are almost certain to secure the monopoly of her trade and with it a market, not only for our silver, but also for our coal and iron, our wheat and Indian corn, our manufactures, our literary and our art products. And moreover we shall inevitably become what England is now, the Occidental world's emporium for Japanese, Chinese, and East India products. Instead of being obliged to go to Europe for these products, as now, Europe will be obliged to come to us for them.

Was it mere forgetfulness or a perversion of correct views which induced some of our public men to entertain even for an instant the notion of abolishing the double standard and degrading our silver product, or was it the sinister advice of nations, whose far-seeing commercial policies detected the advantages which we possessed over them in the future rivalry for the rich trade of the Orient?

Already has the partial demonetization of silver in Europe had the effect of helping to treble the stock of silver which Asia possessed at the opening of this century, and yet so small is the stock of coin among Asiatic nations that, if silver is not entirely demonetized in the Occident, there is not the slightest chance that the surplus silver of the world for centuries to come will suffice for the wants of Asia. Even with a partial demonetization of silver in the Occident, Asia will be able to absorb such portion of the surplus current supplies of the world as can be spared, as well as a large portion of the stock, without being saturated with silver.

SILVER CANNOT BECOME CHEAPER THAN IT IS AT PRESENT.

To those who indulge the insane fear that the late decline of silver caused by European demonetization will continue, it is only necessary to say that the thing is impossible. This decline cannot continue after the discarded stock of silver is worked off, and when the cost of its production again becomes the principal factor of its price. And should this country wisely conclude at this favorable juncture of affairs to remonetize silver, the time necessary for it to advance to its former relation with gold, would be comparatively short.

Specie is too scarce in China and India, prices are too low, and the mere maintenance of their present stock of coin demands a supply of many millions a year. I have seen the Humboldt, Truckee and other rivers which flow between the eastern slope of the Sierra Nevadas and the western walls of the Wahsatch, and which, near their sources in the mountains, flow in great volume, sink all at once into the sands of the desert and disappear from view forever. An attempt to saturate Asia with silver, would, to my mind, be as successful as one to saturate the great American desert with the waters of these rivers.

But let us suppose, for the sake of argument, that Asia cannot take the surplus silver of the Occidental world and demands gold instead for the balance of her foreign trade. Would this not make gold so scarce as to force us of the Occident to keep our own stock of silver which we now would banish? And if it would force us to keep it then, why should we not keep it now? Why change and disturb prices only to come to the same result at last? Why place ourselves in a dilemma either horn of which is dangerous? Why attempt to banish silver to Asia or force her to send it back to us, which she would do in case the above supposition be well founded; a supposition not borne out either by philosophy or fact.

Banish silver from the western world, and you will help to banish progress with it; you will unwittingly and powerfully assist the growth and development of China and India at the expense of our own progress, and precipitate a monetary revolution whose overwhelming and widespread effects no man can fully estimate or foresee.

THE MEXICAN AND CENTRAL AND SOUTH AMERICAN TRADES.

Similar considerations, scarcely less important, demand that our double standard shall be restored in respect of our commercial and other relations with Mexico and Central and South America. All these countries, except Brazil and Chili, have either the single silver standard or the double standard of gold and silver. Omitting Brazil and Chili, these countries contain an aggregate population of more than 25,000,000 souls. This vast population is at the present time entering upon an unprecedented era of activity and progress. Their trade with the manufacturing States of the world belongs naturally and by reason of proximity, to the United States. Shall we run the risk of losing it by unnecessarily depressing the quotations of South American products in our markets, as we should do if we limited ourselves to a single gold standard? Shall we offer to them for their productions a stinted measure of the metal which they do not want, instead of a fair measure of the metal which they do want? Shall we force them to manufacture for themselves, rather than purchase the fabrics they need, from us, in exchange for their valuable raw materials?

THE CRESCENDO AND DIMINUENDO THEORY OF THE ACTION OF MONEY.

I now come to those considerations in reference to this subject which have ever commanded the most serious attention of statesmen and publicists. I allude to the effects of increasing or diminishing money upon the social, moral, and religious welfare of peoples.

I have already shown how profoundly the diminution of coin in the Occidental world, from the period of the Roman empire to that of the discovery or reintroduction of bills of exchange, affected the welfare of Europe. But as, perhaps, it may be disputed that the Dark Ages, and the awful social wretchedness which characterized them, are attributable wholly, or even in great part, to the diminution of money which occurred during that period, I have deemed it best to bring into view more recent and familiar eras of similar character, eras which pertain, not like the Dark Ages, to a remote period and an entire continent, but to later times and particular countries, wherein the relation of the mutations of the currency to the welfare of the people is so close as to admit of little doubt, concerning the influence and action of one upon the other.

I have already stated that, from the nature and function of money, it made no difference to the welfare or convenience of society whether the total sum of money was large or small, provided that it was neither so large nor so small that the substance of which it was made, the precious metals, could practically be coined into pieces of convenient size for transportation or handling, and for the transactions of the ordinary business of life.

While this is quite true, it nevertheless does make a most important difference whether the sum of money be increasing or diminishing. This difference, and the social phenomena connected with it, has been very fitly termed by the author of the Essay on Currency in the original edition of Johnson's Cyclopedia, the *Crescendo* and *Diminuendo* theory, a phrase derived from the terminology of music, an art whose terms are essentially expressive of movement in time.

SOCIAL EFFECTS OF INCREASING AND DIMINISHING MONEY.

Crescendo or increasing, and *diminuendo* or diminishing, are terms which have been deemed convenient for the expression of the movement of the stock of money in time. While this stock is increasing, prices rise; exchange or commerce is stimulated; new enterprises are set afoot; the products of agriculture, manufactures, and mining are increased; the commercial and industrial classes find abundant employment, and earn remunerative profits and wages; bankruptcies and suicides rarely happen; marriages are promoted; the newly-born survive in greater numbers; population increases in quicker ratio; letters, the fine arts, and the sciences make most rapid strides; education, intelligence, morality, and the observance of religion are promoted; and the general happiness of mankind becomes greatly enhanced.

What is the cause of all this industrial activity and social progress? What action or influence of the increasing stock of money lies at the bottom of it? Simply this: that an increasing stock of money tends to distribute wealth, and it is the distribution of wealth which effects these wonderful results. "Oh! it is agrarianism or communism that you propose? You would go on increasing artificially and by legislation (for it is only artificially that it can be done) the sum of the currency forever, in order that wealth may be continually distributed, industrial activity stimulated, and social progress promoted."

I propose nothing of the sort. I have depicted the consequences of an increasing stock of money, not in order to advocate an artificially increasing currency, but as preliminary to depicting the consequences of an artificially diminishing currency, and with the view of warning the country against submitting to any such diminution. I do not propose to rob the capitalist; but neither do I propose to permit the capitalist to rob society.

Whilst the stock of money is diminishing prices fall; commerce is depressed; enterprises are abandoned or neglected; industry is paralyzed; its products are diminished; its supporters defeated in their just expectations or thrown out of employment; bankruptcies and forced sales are increased; marriages are discouraged; suicides become common; the newly-born perish; the increase of population is retarded; the cultivation of letters is abandoned; the arts and sciences fall into decay; education, intelligence, morality and religion are neglected; crime increases; and general misery prevails.

What is the connection between the stock of money and these appalling social phenomena? Simply this: that a diminishing stock of money tends to concentrate wealth, and the concentration of wealth is a cause sufficient to promote all of these evils. "Would you, then, legislate with the view of preventing the stock of money from being decreased? Would you repeat those measures of medieval coercion which distinguished the reign of Henry V, who forbade gold or silver to be used in the arts in order to prevent the stock of money from being diminished?"

I would do nothing of the sort. I propose neither to increase the currency by artificial means nor to diminish it by coercion. I propose to follow and advocate that policy which little minds never perceive the advantage of pursuing, but which the great men of the world have recognized to be the only safe one in commercial affairs. I propose to let things alone. *Laissez faire* in money is as important to the well being of the world as *laissez faire* in corn.

Is it not time, Mr. President, that we republicans, we the exemplars of civil freedom to the world, should abandon and renounce this mischievous policy of meddling with the affairs of commerce; this policy which has been handed down to us by the tyrants and marplots of the world; the men with bloody hands and the men with ruthless purposes? Is it not time that we practiced freedom as well as preached it?

For five thousand years has the world been amassing a stock of gold and silver money wherewith to conduct its commerce, and yet in one instant and by a single blow, would our irreverant and mischievous hands annihilate one half of this stock. The act of 1873 essentially impaired the character of silver as money in this country, a character which it did not owe to legislation, but to fitness and immemorial usage. Could the act have affected other countries as it did this one alone, it would have demonetized silver throughout the world.

What is the principal effect of demonetizing silver? It reduces the entire stock of money by one-half. This effect may be mitigated by permitting a small sum of debased silver coins, as tokens, to pass current for petty payments in each country, but even then its chief harm remains. The money of the world commences to diminish; prices fall; wealth becomes centralized and concentrated in a few hands; property is sacrificed to pay debts incurred before the diminution; bankruptcies ensue; industry is petrified; want and wretchedness stare the commercial classes in the face, and to escape from these disasters they take refuge in dishonesty and immorality, and in the end wind up with crime and destruction.

The evidence of these deplorable consequences of arbitrarily diminishing the stock of money is to be found in the social statistics of all countries. It is only for the sake of brevity that I content myself with adducing a portion of those only of this country. And here let me remark to the possible objection that the statistics of the currency of the United States include paper promises, that the principle is the same, whether the currency is of money alone or money and paper combined. So long as the promises are deemed to be good enough to pass current as money their effect upon prices is precisely the same. It does not follow from this, as some theorists erroneously maintain, that paper promises would pass current as money without a money basis. On the contrary, repeated experience proves that they will not. Nor does it follow that, because a diminishing stock of money or mixed currency produces the evils alluded to that these evils can be avoided by recourse to a forced currency of paper. They can only be avoided by letting the currency alone, and the sooner we learn and appreciate the importance of this great truth the better will it be for our country and the world at large.

[For the tables alluded to in the text, see Appendix.]

THE WORLD'S STOCK OF THE PRECIOUS METALS THE GREAT CONSERVATOR OF ITS CIVILIZATION.

It will perhaps be remarked that, no statistical evidence has been offered to support the assertion made with regard to the effect of the movement of the currency upon letters, the arts, etc. The reason for this is that, while statistics have made such progress that they now fully cover certain features of civilization, and concerning these features afford most thorough and convincing testimony, they do not yet fully cover certain other features, such as those omitted from the illustrations adduced. Within the boundaries to which thus far its conquests have been confined, the use of statistics is of the highest importance, to the student, the publicist, and the legislator; beyond that, such use is almost valueless, and want of discrimination as to where to stop in the employment of statistical evidence, can have but the single result of bringing statistics into undeserved disrepute.

We know *a priori*, that the gradual diffusion of wealth means also the gradual diffusion of the work of life, wherein no feudal tyrant or merciless plutocrat can lord it over the masses of a community bound to exacting toil or hopeless slavery. It is only during this tendency (mark, I say tendency) toward a distribution of rewards according to effort that letters and the arts can flourish. At all other periods, if they make any progress at all, it is confined to a few favored persons, and soon perishes; for the acquisition of letters must be the result of leisure and exemption from toil, and the community that is bound to continual labor can never hope to enjoy the fruits of this divine art.

Therefore such an increment of the stock of money as would work out a gradual diffusion of wealth, and with it the more equitable distribution of work and leisure than would result from a stock of money which was decreasing or stationary while population advanced, could not fail, and it has never yet failed, to promote the progress of letters, the arts and sciences, morality and religion. Nor could any greater increment occur than one which would be sufficient to induce a *gradual* diffusion of wealth; that is, so long as the world retained its present vast stock of the precious metals. Estimating this stock at $5,700,000,000, it requires $85,500,000 a year to keep it from waste by abrasion and loss, and the annual supply of the precious metals or so much of them as is available for coin has rarely been so much in excess of this sum as to be sufficient to produce more than a very inconsiderable and gradual diffusion of wealth. If the increase by population be considered, the process would be extremely slow.

Viewed from this point, it will be seen that the world's stock of the precious metals has really been the great Conservator of Civilization. It is this stock and its slow increment since the sixteenth century, which has kept prices, on the whole, steady and slowly rising; just as it was the decrement of this stock which threatened the extinction of civilization during the Middle Ages. It was the little of it that survived throughout that memorable era which prevented the total subversion of society, and with it letters and the arts, in a word, civilization, and it was in the country that preserved the greatest stock of it during that period that civilization held aloft its highest torch.*

THE RESERVOIR OF THE PRECIOUS METALS.

Lest this phrase, "the great Conservator of Civilization," sounds too grand, let it be supposed that at the present time no reservoir of the precious metals existed, or that the entire stock of money was destroyed in an instant. Setting aside the incalculably calamitous consequences of such a catastrophe, is it not plain that the annual supply of the metals, now amounting to about one hundred millions, would assume a new importance in the distribution of wealth and each individual's share of production. Assuming that the precious metals would continue to be used for money, because no other materials would answer the purpose so well, would not these supplies, as fast as they came forward, affect the prices of commodities and services so enormously and suddenly as virtually to place society at the mercy of the few persons who might be able to control or anticipate such supplies?

---

*Prof. John W. Draper, in his recent work entitled "The Conflict between Science and Religion," states that Almansor, the Moorish king of Grenada, then the foremost country of Europe in civilization, population, and wealth, left at his death a treasure of gold and silver amounting in value to $150,000,000. How much of this sum consisted of coin is not stated.

In the immensity of the world's stock of the precious metals, which forms a measure of value of such vast proportions that no vicissitudes of production can sensibly affect it, society therefore possesses a guarantee for the conservation of all those institutions upon which civilization depends; upon diffusion of wealth, adequate reward for effort, due proportion of production, liberty, leisure, letters, the arts, morality, and religion. And yet it is one half of this precious stock that madmen would now destroy or degrade to the level of gewgaws and bangles.

In the face of the significant facts which we have found to correspond with the movement of the currency, whether in the same is counted only the real money in circulation, or the real money combined with the credits based upon it, (if due allowance be made for their differing ratios of activity,) I ask you, are you prepared to confirm and ratify the thoughtless act of 1873, which demonetized silver as a legal tender in the United States, or will you restore that metal to its rightful position in the money of the country?

Have the industrial, the commercial, the active, the progressive, the working classes of the country, no rights that legislation is bound to respect? What authority has this Chamber to shorten or curtail the standard by which their labor is to be measured? What justice, what wisdom, what safety is there in assisting to destroy the efficiency of one-half of the world's stock of specie, one-half of that measure of value which has come down to us sanctified by fifty centuries of toil, of usage, of experiment, of universal approval? Can you look on with unconcern and permit the entire relations of society to be disturbed in the fancied interests of that small class of persons, who in every country are wealthy enough to monopolize the possession of its measure of value—which, at best, is limited, and barely sufficient to keep pace with the increase of population and commerce?

Such is the pressing scarcity of money, both of gold and silver, throughout the world, that every conceivable form of substitute for it, both safe and unsafe, is in use to eke it out. Every country of the world is using credit in some form as a temporary substitute for money; yet you would arbitrarily demonetize one-half the stock of money, under the erroneous impression, either that one metal is a measure of value less fluctuating than two, or the equally erroneous one that the option of two metals to pay with is derogatory to the rights of creditors which accrued while that option was open.*

CONSTITUTIONAL AND LEGAL ASPECTS OF THE CASE.

I shall now endeavor to show that under our Constitution both the precious metals are made legal tender for the payment of debts.

I hold—

1st. That the word "money," as used in article one, section eight, of the "Constitution for the United States," means both the precious metals, silver and gold, and, by reason of the context, cannot mean either paper promises or one of the metals only.

2d. That the power to "regulate the value thereof" was necessary in order to render this meaning effective, and

---

*The main argument used in favor of the gold valuation is this: "If a creditor, having stipulated for a fixed payment, may be paid by the debtor in either gold or silver, the latter chooses the material which comes cheapest to him, and the creditor suffers an injustice." Without inquiring whether the creditor on entering upon the contract also exercised his option in furnishing the debtor with either material, and therefore cannot claim another treatment—without inquiring whether, as he can also part with the material received on the same terms, and must do so, I can show you that the dogma is one untrue, both in practice and in theory. * * * The large business of exchanging contracts, as well as all such dealings in capital and commodities, in which the "creditor" stands in the position assumed above, is carried on by accounts, checks, and clearing systems without the use of any currency, and so the great system depends upon the exchange of equivalents of value alone. * * * There can be no question of any difference or disproportionate "cheapness" between them, (the metals.) The debtor, in order to obtain either gold or silver coin, must render up the same equivalent for either. (Ernest Seyd, Journal of the Royal Society of Arts, March 10, 1876, p. 320.)

that, had "money" meant one metal instead of two the power to regulate value would have been supererogatory, abortive, and absurd.

3d. That no other construction of the phrase "to regulate the value thereof" is admissible, because even in theory law cannot regulate values, unless the things whose values are to be regulated are specified, and, practically, unless also, the law-power or Government possesses control of the supply or demand of the things to be valued. As all things cannot be specified, and as Government only has control of the supply of gold and silver coins, it follows that the value of these commodities, one to the other, is all that can be "regulated" under the Constitution, and that this regulation constitutes both silver and gold as money and legal tender.

I. Article one, section eight, of the Constitution for the United States provides that "the Congress shall have power * * * * to coin money, regulate the value thereof, and of foreign coin, and fix the standard of weights and measures."

What is money? Gold and silver coined. This was the only meaning attached to "money" when the Constitution was framed, and it is the only proper meaning. In late days the word, money, has been used to mean any circulating media, whether gold or silver coined, or promises to pay. That such is not the meaning of the term as employed in the Constitution is evident from the phrase "to coin," which prefixes the word, "money." Promises to pay cannot be coined, nor were any other metals than gold and silver used as money in this country or any other at the period of the Constitution; therefore, money, as mentioned in that instrument meant gold and silver coined, and could not have meant anything else.

Nor could it have meant either one of these metals separately, because of the affix, "and regulate the value thereof."

What is value? The relation between two services or commodities exchanged, or, to be more precise, the quantitative relation in services or commodities between two services or commodities exchanged. I have already explained the meaning of this term. (See p. 19, *ante*.) It must not be compared with worth, utility, or desirability, which are intrinsic qualities or characteristics without quantity; whilst value is an extrinsic and a quantitative characteristic which is only determinable in exchange. Worth, utility, and desirability may reside in an object without reference to exchange. Value without exchange is impossible. Law cannot regulate the worth, utility, or desirability of a commodity. Why? Because these are intrinsic and incommensurable characteristics, and are, therefore, not susceptible of regulation. Law can regulate value, because value is an extrinsic characteristic, determinable by exchange. But law cannot regulate the value of a commodity generally, and as to all things, unless it specifies separately the quantity of all things which shall be interchangeable. This is not only palpably impracticable, but, even were it practicable, is clearly inadmissible as a construction of the constitutional phraseology. An attempt to regulate the value of money as to all things would produce the utmost injustice and confusion in industrial affairs, and entirely subvert the Constitution and the objects for which it was established. The power to regulate the value of money was therefore confined to gold and silver only. It could not have been with reference to other things.

II. Even with reference to gold and silver, the power to regulate the value of money would have been supererogatory unless money meant both gold and silver, and value the relation between them; for value in respect to an isolated thing is inconceivable and impossible, value being a relation and not an intrinsic quality. If "money," according to the Constitution, meant both gold and silver, the power to regulate the value thereof was a necessary incident to that of coinage, and this view affords the only explanation of the employment of the phrase "to regulate the value thereof" in the Constitution. Otherwise the phrase was powerless, meaningless, and absurd. To coin money and regulate the value thereof are, therefore, inseparable powers, and although Congress is not required to exercise them, but is merely permitted to do so, yet, if exercised, they can only be exercised together, and the exercise of one power without the other is unconstitutional. Therefore, so long as any coins of the United States are in existence the suppression of the silver dollar by the act of 1873 is void.*

III. Practically, the Government has control of only two commodities among all those known to the world: these two are gold and silver coins. The Constitution gives to the Government exclusively the power to coin money, and this power gives it practical control over the supply of gold and silver coins. It may be held, indeed, that the same power gives it also control over any substances which it may choose to employ as money, for example, copper, tobacco, musket-balls, wampum-peag, paper promises, etc. But the impracticability of regulating the value of substances of such heterogeneous composition and limitless supply merely serves to show the absurdity of attempting to extend the meaning of the phrase "money" beyond that which was clearly attached to it at the time of the Constitution, viz: gold and silver coins. These various substances, and many others, had all been employed in this country as substitutes for money, or as tokens, previous to the Constitution, and some of them were in wide use at the time of that instrument. But it is quite clear that none of them were referred to in the phrase "money," and that gold and silver alone were meant.

Having control of the two commodities, gold and silver coins, and of these two only, it was not and is not practicable for the Government of the United States to regulate the value as between any other commodities than gold and silver coins.†

---

*The word dollar was first defined in the coinage act of April 1792. Therefore, the powers of coining and regulating value were first exercised together. There was no regulation of value before coining: therefore no regulation of the value of the foreign coins which circulated in the United States previous to 1792.

†Not even between gold and silver bullion.

Having made this regulation, Congress went as far as it had power to go. In the regulation that "the proportional value of gold to silver in all coins which shall by law be current as money within the United States, shall be as fifteen to one, according to quantity in weight of pure gold or pure silver," (Act of April 2, 1792, section 11,) Congress exercised all the kind of power which was conferred upon it by the Constitution regarding the regulation of values.

VIEWS OF THE LAST GENERATION ON THE CONSTITUTIONAL QUESTION.

The view herein taken is that which has hitherto been taken by all who have carefully considered this subject. In a report to this Chamber by one of its members, Mr. Sanford, the chairman of a "Select Committee to consider the State of the Currency," appointed by the 21st Congress, (see Ex. Doc., 2d Session, 21st Cong., Dec. 15, 1830,) he held the following language:

> "The Constitution of the United States evidently contemplates in the power conferred upon this Government to coin money, regulate the value thereof, and of foreign coins, and the restriction imposed on the States, to make nothing but gold and silver coins a tender in payment of debts, that the money of this country shall be gold and silver. Our system of money established in the year 1792, fully adopts the principle that it is expedient to coin and use both metals as money, and such has always been the opinion of the people of the United States."

At this period (1830) there was not a dollar of gold in the country. England had nearly depleted us of what little we had previous to 1817, in order to prepare for the resumption of specie payments, which had been suspended in England since 1797, and which resumption the ruling classes of England had unwisely or selfishly planned upon the basis of a single metal. This depletion went on from 1817 until after 1820, perhaps until 1821 or 1822. Then it stopped, so far as we were concerned, from sheer exhaustion on our part. We had no more gold to sell. At that period we had nearly $70,000,000 of bank paper afloat. What condition this country would have been left in, had our statesmen been as indifferent then as they appear to have been in 1873, in regard to the constitutional requirement to make both gold and silver legal tender money, I leave to the imagination. Our population was then 10,000,000. We had but lately emerged from a war with England, at the close of which gold had stood, in our excessive paper issues, at 117, and an attempt to resume in 1817 was met by a revulsion in 1819, and a secondary revulsion in 1821.

Imagine 10,000,000 of people, exhausted by war and the sores of a double revulsion, depleted of every dollar of gold, and divested of the power to resume in silver or use that metal in the payment of debts. Do you suppose, if the statesmen of 1822 had been as forgetful of the interests of their country and as oblivious of constitutional law as seem to have been those of 1873, that any respect would have been paid to their legislation, and that if it had been respected, the country could have been saved from revulsion and repudiation? I fancy not.

And this episode of our history conveys more than one warning, more than the warning that monometalism, if persisted in, may bring the country to great social and political disturbances. Some people are so filled with the sense of security that a warning of repudiation seems to them a mere bugaboo. Simple failure in an attempt to resume specie payments is, to them, an event of far greater likelihood, if not of importance. Very well, then; the episode before us contains the warning of such a failure; of two such failures. We tried to resume in 1817; we tried again in 1821; and on both occasions distress followed. What was the cause? Lack of specie. We tried to redeem sixty or seventy millions of paper with twenty or twenty-five millions of coin. What was the cause of the lack of specie? England had drained us of our gold, which she virtually overvalued in order to prepare for her own resumption.

But for silver, the use of which as legal tender had been

preserved for us by the Constitution, we should not have resumed at all, at least not for forty years after, when California opened. The case is similar now. England again has drained us of our gold. We have $800,000,000 of paper afloat, and less than $50,000,000 of specie wherewith to redeem it. Yet Congress orders resumption to take place, and forbids the employment of silver wherewith to resume. Is it not plain that resumption is quite impracticable; that a sum of gold sufficient for the purpose cannot be purchased throughout the world at any prices for bonds or exports at which we would be willing to sell; and that any attempt to resume, unless the constitutional requirements as to the monetization of silver are obeyed, will plunge the country into all the disasters of monetary revulsion?

VESTED INTERESTS UNDER THE CONSTITUTION.

Ever since Mr. Webster's time it has been an oft-quoted doctrine that under the Constitution the destruction or impairment of a vested interest by act of Government is in the nature of a breach of contract. Without giving adhesion to this doctrine, it ought to be remarked that, as a rule of law it appears to work too many ways to be practicable, because legislation is *impossible* without disturbance of social relations, and therefore, of existing interests. However this may be, the rule has been held to apply with peculiar force, though I know not why, to the vested interests of the public creditor, and prejudice has been arrayed against the return to the double standard, because it is held that payments in silver might affect the interests of the public creditor. To this I have already adverted and I do not propose to raise that question now. But while on the subject of vested interests and breach of contract there is something more to be said. That something relates to the mining interests of this country, interests which, I think it will be admitted, are quite as important to the welfare of the country as those of the public creditor.

The mining interests of this country came into existence under clauses of the Constitution which it was well understood made both gold and silver money legal tender for the payment of debts. During the first three-quarters of the period of our national existence, silver chiefly and for the most time only was employed as money; during the last quarter of the period gold was chiefly so employed. But not until 1873 (and that merely by implication) was either metal demonetized. It was therefore while both metals were money that the entire gold and silver mining interests of this country were created and built up, at first upon alluvial findings and washings, and afterward with the profit from those upon the more difficult and expensive ores in veins and lodes. These interests, once so few, now so numerous that they yearly throw into the lap of the country $100,000,000 of the precious metals, more than one-half of the product of the entire world, and sufficient, if rightly managed, to render our country the clearing house of the world, were literally built up with the naked fingers, with the rude pick and cradle. This single foundation was that clause of the Constitution which makes the precious metals money, but for which they would have had no existence, and upon the continued and faithful observance of which they depend even to-day for maintenance, because though of gigantic dimensions in the aggregate their average profit is so small that it vanishes with the slightest disturbance in the value of the precious metals. Yet there are those who hold in respect of these permanent, important, and well deserving interests vested in mining, that the interests of a pack of clamorous money-lenders in London, Berlin, and Frankfort are of vastly more account than theirs. The recent project of a Boston correspondent to pay the interest on the public debt in silver dollars they sneered at as "a nice down-east joke," and bullied about the rights of vested interests under the Constitution.

The Constitution! Sir, when I come to pronounce that word I do so with a respect that is akin to reverence; for under the shadow of that instrument, so wisely and so wondrously drawn as to have lasted a century of the World's busiest times, there has grown up from thirteen feeble and jealous colonies, containing 3,000,000 people of varied origin and conflicting interests, a nation of thirty-eight proud States, containing 45,000,000 people, free, homogeneous, prosperous, strong, and progressive. When and where else in the World's history has such a growth been seen? The constitution of the Roman republic, though nominally it lasted longer, really did not last so long, for it was frequently and essentially altered and modified. It had to deal with a far lesser number of States, interests, or people, and the progress under it was nothing as compared with our progress. Take the most important of modern States, England, France, or Germany. In which of them will you find the same freedom, the same equality, the same ingenuity and adaptability, the same energy, the same elasticity, the same rapidity of growth, either in numbers or wealth? Since the date of our Constitution England has scarcely trebled her population. France has not yet doubled hers, while ours has increased fifteen times. Our national life has not been without its vicissitudes, but who can deny that it has been grand, noble, and progressive, and that it is due all of it to that sacred instrument which we rightly term the Constitution for the United States.

In pronouncing the name of this instrument I do so with the respect due to the mighty agency which it has had in building up a great nation and promoting the progress of man in all countries.

In this remembrance I should almost regard it as sacrilege to invoke its support of a false doctrine, to twist it, distort it, or seek to turn it aside from its plain meaning. And I regard it as sacrilege when I see it used as a cover to protect the sharp-toothed greed of plutocracy.

That gold and silver are both the money of the Constitution is so obviously the meaning of that instrument that the question, so far as I am aware, was never fully raised until lately and after the passage of the act of 1873. That the Constitution either directly or by the remotest implication throws any mantle of protection over the public creditor, which does not at the same time as amply cover the third greatest industrial interest of the whole country —this I deny.

Between an interest which has become "vested" by dint of hasty and ill-considered legislation, and one which has become "vested" through bold adventure, the peril of life, the miasma of death-inclosing valleys, the snows of lofty mountains, the arid and burning plains, through incessant labor, and far away from "home" and familiar faces—between these classes of vested interests there is a wide difference. One of these classes demands the maintenance of the act of 1873, because it fears that the overthrow of that act may have some possible bearing upon the advantages which it has secured; the other asks for its immediate abolition because it is unconstitutional, it is unwise, it is sapping the foundation of an industry of vital importance to the country. Let the Senate decide between them, and choose whether it will intrust the welfare of the nation rather to the money-dealers of Lombard street and the Continent than to the hardy mountaineers of the Sierra Nevadas, whose occupations are environed with danger and whose unceasing watch-word is Liberty!

WHAT THE HAND OF THE DESTROYER HATH SPARED.

Some of the greatest nations of the earth have been destroyed, and it has been asserted that nothing remains to attest their existence except the language they employed. Such is the case with the ancient Arabians, the Phœnicians, and the Carthaginians, who were all of the same race. Such, also, was the case with the ancient Malays, Egyptians, and Toltecs. Of the Lake Dwellers of Switzerland or the Mound Builders of America, it is said that not even language remains. And yet all of these nations and many other prehistoric ones, as the Pelasgians, the Etruscans, etc., have left a legacy to mankind. That legacy is the precious metals which they employed for money. Much of it must still be in existence in some form or other of usefulness. The hand of the destroyer, Time, hath spared this, even while he hath not spared language. And yet there are impious men to-day, who, for the sake of a temporary personal advantage, would strike down this last and precious vestige of nations who fought and labored scores of centuries ago that we might now live in peace and plenty.

WORSE THAN DESTROYING THE MINES.

The demonetization of silver would not merely have the same result as the stoppage of all the silver mines of the world; the result would be far worse: it would be as though one-half of all the labor of past ages, except what doubtful legacy has remained in the shape of land improvements, were blotted out of existence. This would be worse than destroying the mines; for they might be reopened, whereas the demonetized metal would be irretrievably lost in the arts and otherwise.

"LET THINGS STAND AS THEY ARE."

"Let things stand as they are" is the false and treacherous maxim of those who have wrongfully obtained an advantage over others. *Laissez faire* does not mean "let things stand as they are," but "let alone" altogether. The existing state of affairs may be the result of a good deal of meddlesomeness. To let them remain as they are would be to let ruin work its own way. The single standard foisted upon this nation by the act of 1873 was a mischievous interference with trade, and things cannot be let alone until this act is repealed. The suppression of the double standard cannot be compared with the usury laws. It is ten thousand times, nay, infinitely worse; for in the rate of interest for money there is competition between money-lenders, whereas, concerning the kind of metal in which they will demand to be paid, there will be no competition whatever. Herein the interests of all money lenders are identical. The only way to meet their rapacity is by restoring the double standard, to give the debtor the same option in paying that the creditor had in lending.

ANTIQUITY OF MONEY—PREHISTORIC NATIONS—EXPERIMENTS IN MONEY—GOLD STANDARD—PLATINUM COINS.

Hitherto, in alluding to the antiquity of gold and silver money, I have sometimes used the expression thirty or fifty centuries, the former referring to the oldest coins now extant, the latter to the earliest period for which we have indisputable evidence concerning the use of these metals for money. But if there is any credence to be reposed in the numerous authorities quoted in Baldwin's "Prehistoric Nations," both gold and silver were employed as money by the ancient Arabians or Cushites, from sixty to a hundred centuries ago. The precise antiquity of money is, however, of little consequence in this connection. It is sufficient if we know that it is of very great antiquity, and of this there is no doubt whatever.

During all this time every conceivable sort of experiment was made with money. It was tried in ingots, in "dust," in wire coils, and in coins; round, square, oblong, punctured, buttoned, milled, and unmilled coins; coins with and without alloy; pure coins, composite coins, base coins, plated coins, coins of brass, tin, iron, nickel, and platinum.

The history of platinum coins exemplifies the results of all these experiments. These coins were adopted in Russia in 1826, during the notable decline in the product of the precious metals, which occurred from 1810 to 1840, and before the Ural and Siberian mines were opened. No substance was intrinsically more suitable to answer the purposes of money than platinum. It was only inferior to the precious metals in one respect; but that respect proved fatal to its continuance. There was no great stock of platinum in the world to modify the vicissitudes of its current production as there is of the precious metals; no reservoir of antiquity; no heirloom of the centuries. Consequently, every time the annual production of platinum greatly increased, prices in platinum coins were suddenly and violently advanced, and every time the production of platinum fell off, prices fell. These violent aberrations proved fatal to the continued use of this metal for coins, and it was discontinued. The same thing had previously occurred with coins of brass, iron, tin, etc., and if our nickel coins were anything more than tokens, mere promises to pay stamped on base metal, the same thing would happen with them.

Substitutes for money form another class of experiments which have ended disastrously in bank panics, in commercial crises, in stay-laws, and in repudiation. The trouble is the same with bank credits as with coins of any other substances than the precious metals. There is no stock on hand to modify the influence of great supplies.

The adoption of the single gold standard is another experiment in money of similar character, and subject in a measure to the same fatal objection. In this case the stock on hand is very great; but it is only one-half as much as that of the two precious metals combined; and this important fact must settle the fate of the experiment.

COMPARATIVE FACILITY AND COST OF TRANSPORTING GOLD AND SILVER.

During the great Continental wars of three-fourths of a century ago, the necessity of having large military chests in the service of armies rendered it necessary to transport large sums of specie in the field. For this purpose gold was found to be superior to silver on account of its lighter weight in proportion to value. While the fact was then so important that it may have had no little influence in reconciling the British nation with that formal adoption of the single gold standard which followed shortly after these wars, it is now of no importance whatever, even in

Europe, and never has been of any importance in this country. Armies do not employ military chests now-a-days. Russia, Austria, Italy, Germany, France, and even England, have fought their greatest campaigns with the aid of treasury or bank paper. In America all our wars have been fought with paper. The colonial Expedition to Louisbourg, in 1745, was conducted with paper, our war of Independence was fought with paper, our Rebellion was put down with paper. Whatever may be the evil effects of paper, it is hopeless to expect that it will not be issued by Governments in the event of great wars. War is of itself the greatest of evils, and the lesser evil of paper merely follows in its wake, as sharks do the mutinous ship.

In times of peace the cost of transporting a given sum in gold or silver is the same, notwithstanding the lighter weight of the former. Freights upon gold and silver are rated according to value, and not according to bulk or weight. The freight upon a ton of gold from California to New York is now more than sixteen times as much as that upon a ton of silver, and this is the same upon railway, and steamship, and other transportation lines throughout the world. The curious will find the actual freights quoted in M. Cernuschi's work on Bi-metalism.

The rating of freights upon gold and silver by value instead of bulk or weight is due to the important consideration of risk. The bulk or weight of a million dollars in silver is far greater than that of a million dollars in gold; but the risk of loss from accident or robbery is far greater in the case of gold than in that of silver. An ingot of gold worth $2,000 could be very easily lost, and would be very difficult to recover in case of a railway collision, a fire, the breaking of a bridge, a robbery, etc. An ingot of silver worth $2,000 would be difficult to lose and easy to recover; nor could a thief conveniently carry it off, because it would weigh over a hundred pounds. No guards are required to conduct a shipment of silver bars because no highwaymen could lift them, while gold ingots of the same value could be stowed away in the pocket, and therefore have to be guarded by armed men. The expense incurred in this and other ways fully counterbalances the saving which arises from inferior bulk or weight in transportation.

As to the alleged superiority of gold in handling sums of money suitable for the ordinary payments of commercial life, it is the merest moonshine. One would suppose, to hear this claim made, that such an institution as banking was unknown to the world, instead of being, what is the fact, of seven hundred years' growth. Only the most narrow theorist will contend that the resumption of specie payments in this country will be followed by the extinction of banks. After resumption banks will receive specie on deposit and issue bills in its place, and these bills will be used for payments from hand to hand, just as similar bills were used before suspension. The only difference will be that, thanks to the superiority of the national over the old State bank systems, the bills will be better secured, indeed, we may say, absolutely secured, provided, of course, that no relaxation is made of the admirable and sound conditions and principles upon which this system was founded; and of such relaxation we need entertain no fears.

In such case, and in all cases, we always have a perfect expedient to obviate the inconvenience of handling coins, that of depositing the coins with the Government, which shall issue therefor, dollar for dollar, bills to be declared by law receivable for all payments, public and private.

This project I need not elaborate at this time or in this connection. Its suggestion merely serves to show that in any event our money, whether of gold or silver, or both, as it should be, can always be made easy enough to handle, through the medium of representative paper.

It should always be borne in mind that, as M. Cernuschi remarks, a bill of exchange (or bank note) for silver does not weigh any more than one for gold.

THE SINGLE STANDARD COMMERCIALLY UNPROFITABLE.

If we look at the question from the national and not

merely the plutocratical point of view, it will appear that every nation which demonetizes one of the metals and limits itself to the use of the other only punishes itself. It would leave more money to the other nations. Prices would fall in the former countries and rise in the latter. The former would have to sell their products to the latter at low prices and purchase back in high prices; just as China sells to us now at low prices and buys from us at high ones. If instead of selling their products wherewith to pay for the products they purchased, the gold standard nations sold their products wherewith to purchase the demonetized metal in which the prices of the other were rated, as for instance, if England purchased silver wherewith to pay for East India products, she would have to purchase such silver at the high prices of commodities which would prevail in India after the surplus stock of Europe were driven thither. In other words, the course of exchange would be against the gold standard nations. For example, a pound sterling of exchange upon India would cost more than a pound sterling of gold in England. Arrange it as you will, either product against product, or product against exchange, the result will be the same. The nations with a limited stock of money would trade disadvantageously with nations having both the metals for their standard of value. This is the secret of the profitableness of the Oriental trade. The Oriental countries employ but one metal for their standard—silver. The Occidental countries have hitherto employed both metals. Hence the low prices of the Orient and high prices of the Occident. As a measure between the labor of the two great divisions of the world, it has always been favorable to the Occident. This advantage it is now proposed to destroy. To call it madness would be but a mild stigma.

OUR MONEY SHOULD BE EN RAPPORT WITH THAT OF THE WORLD.

Having already shown that gold and silver was the money of the world—not gold or silver singly—it would seem hardly necessary to reply more specifically to an objection to the restoration of the double standard which some men suggest. That suggestion is, that unless we adopt the gold standard we shall not be *en rapport* with the standard of England, the country with which we transact the most commerce.

Those who suggest this objection do not appear to remember how foreign exchanges are conducted. Balances of trade are not paid in coin, but in bullion, and it makes no difference whether the bullion is of gold or silver or both. It goes for its value, whatever that may be at the time. Exchanges are adjusted by means of bills, which are rated in view of the standard of value in the several countries upon or through which the bills are drawn. Suppose our standard were of gold, and we had to pay for a balance of trade to China: we would not pay in gold coin, but in bullion, in gold, not at its price in this country, but at its price in all countries. This would be determined by the course of exchange, which is the product of settlements between all commercial nations. So, if our standard were the double one of silver and gold, our balances with England would not be settled in gold and silver coin, but in bullion, at its price in all countries, as determined by the course of exchange. We would settle in bills of exchange, as we do now, as we always have done. So far as this objection goes, the discordance between the standards of two countries is of no consequence whatever. Discordance of standard is only material when it has the effect of locally demonetizing, for a greater or lesser duration of time, an important part of the world's stock of coin, and this can only happen when several important countries unite in demonetizing one of the metals. This is the case now. Silver is being driven to the Orient, and though, in spite of demonetization, it will find its way back in time, yet meanwhile, the nations who unite in demonetizing it will needlessly produce a revolution in prices and the relations of the various classes of society, which may seriously affect the rank of such nations in the scale of civilization.

To render our standard of money *en rapport* with that of England, while it would not prove of the slightest convenience in commercial affairs, would tend to render our institutions of government *en rapport* with hers. If this is what gentlemen desire, they should say so openly, and not under the mask of a fancied commercial advantage. Their constituents will then be better able to appreciate their statesmanship.

GROWING INFLUENCE OF THE WORLD'S STOCK OF SPECIE.

There was a time when the world's stock of specie was so small that the slightest vicissitude in the supply of bullion from the mines was sufficient to cause violent fluctuations in prices and violent changes of fortune. The Feudal System owes no little of its strength and permanence to this fact, for it was the only institution upon which the ruling classes, ecclesiastical and secular, could rely to secure to them their monopoly of wealth. When the Feudal System, through many causes,* began to lose strength, the Mercantile System was adopted to serve the purpose of controlling the flow of specie from one country to another. At the present time the world's stock of specie is so great that the vicissitudes of supply can have but little influence upon prices, and as that stock becomes larger and larger the influence of the supply will become less and less. Another century may see society safely placed beyond the influence of these mutations.

Yet now, upon the threshold of a condition of affairs which must do more to equalize the fortunes of individuals and advance the progress of society than any other, it is proposed to destroy at one blow the work of countless centuries by demonetizing one-half of the world's stock of specie, and the United States are asked to assist in this work of superlative madness and inhumanity. Such a

*The invention of gunpowder, the introduction of bills of exchange, the discovery of America, and establishment of colonies with ample arable lands, &c.

proposition, which could only emanate from men crazed and arrogant with good fortune, is not merely an insult to the genius and institutions of this country; it is a bold and direct attack upon progress, upon civilization, upon liberty. The men who have made it do not merely attack the prosperity of their own countries, they conspire to destroy humanity, they are traitors to society; they have urged a proposition of the most violent and revolutionary character.

NOBODY HURT BY RESTORING THE DOUBLE STANDARD.

I ask gentlemen to point me out one individual who can be injured by restoring the double standard, recoining the silver dollar of 371¼ grains fine, and making it a legal tender for all amounts, as it was before. Point me out one man who would suffer by it. Point me out one product of the country which would be lessened in its gold price by restoring the silver dollar. Point me out one interest imperiled, one sacrifice sustained. On the other hand, I will point you out millions of men who will be ruined if you persist in retaining the gold standard. I will name a thousand products of the country which will continue to fall in price. I will show you a myriad of interests in jeopardy and innumerable sacrifices to be sustained.

THE STOCK OF MONEY MAKES PRICES, AND THE COURSE OF PRICES AFFECTS CIVILIZATION.

Double the world's stock of money to-day, and you will double all prices. Diminish it one-half, and prices will fall one-half. This relation of money and price is axiomatic. You will find it in all the books on political economy. No writer has ever ventured to doubt it; not even Tooke, who doubted everything, even his own opinions.

Price is the expression of the measure of value, which is money. The larger the measure the larger the expression or price; the smaller the measure the smaller the expression or price. Hence, with a large stock of coin in the world, prices would be high; with a small stock, prices would be low. To increase the stock of coin is to enhance prices, alleviate the burdens of the debtor class, and distribute wealth, to decrease it is to lower prices, increase the claims of the creditor class, and concentrate wealth. One result leads to social progress; the other to decay. Every dollar hewn out of the rocks, no matter whom it enriches in the first instance, has an immediate effect in alleviating the general condition of mankind. Every dollar, worn out, lost, or demonetized by plutocratical legislation, tends to lower prices and concentrate wealth, tends to impoverish the needy and enrich the affluent.

The proposition to resume specie payments in this country on the gold standard is tantamount to demonetizing one-tenth of the world's stock of silver or one-twentieth of its entire stock of coin. When the long period which has been required to accumulate this stock is taken into consideration, it is not too much to say that this act will set us back in the command of some of the most important factors of civilization as much as a century of constitutional freedom has set us forward.

THE STANDARD OF VALUE IN VARIOUS COUNTRIES IN 1870.

The standard of value which existed in the various principal countries of the world in 1870 was as follows: population in millions:

Double standard.		Silver standard.		Gold standard.	
Country.	Population.	Country.	Population.	Country.	Population.
United States*	39	India	200	United Kingdom.	31
France	36	China	250	Turkey*	36
Italy*	26	Russia*	82	Brazil*	10
Spain	17	Germany	41	Portugal	4
Belgium	5	Austria*	36	Chili	2
Switzerland	3½	Mexico	9	Australia	2
Greece*	1½	Sweden, Norway	6		
Peru	4	Denmark	2		
New Granada	3	Holland	4		
Equador	1	Central America	2½		

* Specie payments suspended.

AN INTERNATIONAL STANDARD CONVENTION.

It would be desirable for all nations to adopt permanently the same standard of value, and if the same were, as in my opinion it no doubt would be, the double standard, to adopt the same relation between the metals. To effect this object all that is necessary is an international standard convention, which can be called by any one of the great powers, and should be called by the United States. Provision should be made that no other projects but the standard and ratio should be determined upon, and that the nations should vote according to population or wealth, or on a mixed basis consisting of both. For such an international convention, to be called by the United States, there is imminent necessity. I regard this project as likely to lead to results of the highest importance. It may become the forerunner of that federation of the nations of which poets have dreamed and bards have sung. The initial point of such a federation is most fitly the Standard of Value, for this lies at the base of all social and governmental arrangements; it determines the institution of property.

THE PECUNIARY INTEREST OF ENGLAND AND GERMANY IN THE GOLD STANDARD.

In a paper published in the *Journal of the Society of Arts* for March 10, 1876, Mr. Ernest Seyd estimates the amount of foreign debt (governmental, corporative, and other) held in England, Germany, and France, as follows:

England	from	$5,000,000,000	to	$5,500,000,000.
Germany	"	2,750,000,000	"	3,000,000,000.
France	"	2,500,000,000	"	2,750,000,000.

Confining our view to England and Germany only, we shall see how great a present pecuniary interest these countries have in establishing and upholding a single gold standard. According to Mr. Seyd's estimates these two countries alone hold over $8,000,000,000 of foreign debt. By limiting themselves to the single gold standard and endeavoring to influence others nations (our own among the number) to adopt it, they have already succeeded in producing a decline of about 7½ per cent. in the relation of gold and silver, this being the ratio of the difference between 15.63 and 16.69, the average relation of silver to gold in 1872 and 1875 respectively. Now, 7½ per cent. on $8,000,000,000 amounts to no less a sum than $600,000,000, which is the measure of the profit of the British and German plutocracy on the foreign debts they hold. Descending from the principal to the interest on these debts, if we estimate the average annual interest at 6 per cent. per annum, which is certainly within the mark, the difference to these plutocracies between obtaining their interest in gold and obtaining it in silver during the years 1872 and 1875 inclusive has been no less than $36,000,000 per annum. Since the introduction of the Demonetization Act into the American Congress these gentry have gained $108,000,000 by having their interest paid in gold instead of silver. The magnitude of this advantage, every dollar of which has been a clear and gratuitous loss to the debtor nations, is surely enough to account for the vehemence of the plutocratical objection to the double standard. With $36,000,000 a year at stake, there is little wonder that they have succeeded in marshaling to their aid so imposing an array of advocates in the legislatures and the press of the victimized countries from which this extra and gratuitous tribute was drawn.

THE RIGHT TIME TO REHABILITATE THE SILVER DOLLAR.

The right time for us to rehabilitate the silver dollar, to restore the double standard, is not when the necessities of nations shall compel them, as it will compel them all, to go into the market for silver. A simultaneous demand from Germany and the United States alone would put that metal up to 15, perhaps for the time even to 14. The right time for us is now, while silver is temporarily cheap, and no other nation of the Occident is bidding for it. Last month silver stood at 17.82, and already it is up to 17.69.

Before the year has expired it may stand at 15.50. It is dangerous and costly to delay. The present time is therefore the most favorable one which may present itself. Let us not postpone reform until it is too late to accomplish it. European demonetization and an exceptional mine gives us a great advantage. Why should we not use it?

PRACTICAL WORKING OF THE SINGLE STANDARD IN ENGLAND.

When an outflow of specie threatens to occur in England the occurrence is sought to be averted and its effects mitigated by raising the rate of discount at bank. This action at once clogs all financial operations by rendering them expensive and difficult of accomplishment. Raising the rate of discount at bank is like putting the breaks on a railway train; lowering it is like taking the breaks off.

The Bank of England was established in 1694. From that year to the year 1816, a period of 122 years, there were only sixteen changes in the bank rate. This rate never fell below four per cent., and (except in two instances to six) never rose above five per cent. During this period the double standard existed in England. In 1816 the double was changed to the single gold standard. From 1816 to 1847—a period of 31 years—there were sixteen changes in the bank rate; as many as had occurred under the double standard during a period of 122 years. But these changes, numerous as they were, compared with the few that had previously taken place, were few themselves compared with the number that took place after 1847, when the gold product of California began to make itself felt in the markets of the world. From 1847 to 1874, inclusive, a period of twenty-seven years, the number of changes in the Bank of England rate was no less than 223, and the rate fluctuated violently from 2½ to 10 per cent. per annum.

These fluctuations have been ascribed by various writers to various causes, but none of these causes appear to have had so potential an effect as the mutations of the gold production of the world, for these must have operated with peculiar and great force in a country which alone, among all the great countries of the world, had committed itself to so unstable a measure of values as gold.

PRACTICAL WORKING OF THE DOUBLE STANDARD IN FRANCE.

While I have not been able to obtain in time for the present purposes the statistics of the changes in the rate of discount by the Bank of France, my general recollection on the subject enables me to say that these changes have been very few and, except at certain critical financial junctures, they have been unimportant. In a word, the rate of discount charged by this great institution, which is second only to the Bank of England in the magnitude of its resources and operations, has been changed but seldom and slightly from the period of its foundation, in the year 1800, to the present day. Even at the financial junctures alluded to, I am unable to find any record of a higher rate than 6½ per cent., and this occurred during the suspension which followed the Franco-German war. This steadiness of the rate is attributable to the double standard.

THE BANK RATE REGULATES ALL COMMERCIAL OPERATIONS.

The rate of discount at bank not only regulates the outflow of specie; it also very powerfully affects all commercial transactions. It is the price at which money can be borrowed to carry domestic produce, to import and export merchandise abroad, to construct railways and other public improvements, to pay debts, meet maturing obligations, and the like. Every commercial speculation, every financial scheme, is influenced by its fluctuations. It is the merchant's inverse barometer, whose fall indicates prosperity, and whose rise points to bankruptcy and ruin; whilst its modifying influence acts like a breakwater to protect the country from the fierce currents of the financial ocean.

NO SUCH REGULATOR IN THE UNITED STATES.

In the United States there is no National Bank *par*

excellence, no great central institution whose operations govern those of all smaller ones, and at once influence the course of trade. There has been no such institution in this country since 1837. The so-called "national banks" are private institutions, and national only to the extent that they are chartered by the Federal Government, and must conform to its regulations as to securities and circulation. They may each of them charge whatever rate of discount they please within the rate permitted by the laws of the State wherein they are situated. As the legal rate of interest differs in nearly all the States, and the banks are not combined under any single management, there is no uniformity in the rate of interest they charge, and it follows that, except so far as concerns the action of certain prominent banks in the leading financial cities of the country, there is no practical check which can be exerted to restrain or modify a threatened outflow of specie, or any other financial disaster or inconvenience.

THEREFORE THE UNITED STATES LESS ABLE THAN ENGLAND, FRANCE, OR GERMANY TO RUN THE RISKS OF A SINGLE STANDARD.

Hence for the United States to trust its commercial prosperity to the violent hazards of a single standard, would be even more improvident than it has proved in the case of England. That country, in its great National Bank, possesses a "governor" upon whose action it can rely to break the force of sudden and great movements of specie. Even with this "governor," we have seen, in the fluctuations of the rate of interest, how violent these movements have been. France possesses a similar "governor;" so does Germany. The former country has never run the risk of trusting to it in this matter by abandoning the double standard, while the latter, during a contemplated change from the silver to the gold standard, has halted midway at the double standard.

Yet, although quite destitute of that great financial mechanism, even with the aid of which France and Germany hesitate to encounter the great peril which England has invited them to share with her, we of the United States are asked to adopt the single gold standard, and run the risk of immediate shipwreck. This may be sound advice; but I must confess it does not appear to come from people who have evinced any solicitude for the welfare of the country.

OPPOSITE AND UNEXPECTED EFFECTS OF THE FRENCH INDEMNITY.

As a consequence of the victory of Germany over France in 1870, the last-named country was compelled to pay to the first-named, an Indemnity, amounting to the enormous sum of $1,000,000,000. One would naturally have supposed that this indemnity would prove a heavy burden to France, and a source of great prosperity to Germany; but, owing, as it seems to me, chiefly to the retention of the double standard in France, and the attempt to establish the gold standard in Germany, these consequences have been reversed; the burden is upon Germany; the prosperity has fallen to the share of France. The presence of a large stock of silver coin in France enabled that country to raise the enormous indemnity fund from its own people, who offered the Government five times as much as it asked for, and at a low rate of interest. This stock of silver would not have been found in the country but for the retention of the double standard of 1803. The rate at which it was loaned was so low that the country scarcely feels the burden, and its industrial activity has received no check.

Germany, on the other hand, no sooner received the indemnity than she unwisely attempted to follow the short-sighted footsteps of England, and changed her standard of silver to gold. What have been the consequences? Panic, interruption of industry, commercial stagnation, and popular distress. To this distress, Germany, unlike England, cannot afford to turn a deaf ear, for the greatness of the former country depends upon its people, and not like the

the latter, upon its wealth. Already Germany hesitates, and she will soon be obliged to retrace her ill-advised steps. If she does not, it is quite safe to foretell that her efforts to establish the gold standard will do more to alienate from her the affections of her heterogeneous populations than the Land Reforms of Stein and Hardenbergh had done to win them. If such a result as a change from the silver or the double standard to the gold one is the natural result of receiving a great war indemnity, it will be the better for Germany the next time she wins a victory to pay an indemnity rather than receive one.

LEGISLATION ON THE STANDARD OF THE UNITED STATES.

Table showing the various acts of the United States Government authorizing the coinage of silver and gold dollars, or their multiples or fractions, the weight of the same in pure metal, the extent to which the same were made legal tenders for the payment of debts, and the legal relation thus established between silver and gold. Also the London market relation of the metals at the period of the passage of such acts.

Act.	Coins.	Weight of dollar. Troy grains, pure.	Extent of legal tender.	Legal relation.	Approximate London market relation.
April 2, 1792.	Silver dollar.........	371.25	Unlimited.	15.00000 to 1........	About 14.9 to 1
	Gold dollar, multiples of*..........	24.75	Unlimited.		
July 31, 1834.	Silver dollar.........	371.25	Unlimited.	16.00215 to 1......	About 15.8 to 1
	Gold dollar, multiples of.........	23.20	Unlimited.		
July 18, 1837.	Silver dollar *and* fractions of†......	371.25	Unlimited.	15.98837 to 1......	About 15.7 to 1
	Gold dollar, multiples of.............	23.22	Unlimited.		
Feb. 24, 1853.	Silver dollar.........	371.25	Unlimited.	15.98837 to 1......	About 15.3 to 1
	Gold dollar *and* multiples of......	23.22	Unlimited.		
	Silver dollar, fractions of...............	345.60	Five dollars.	-	-
Act Feb. 12, 1873, Rev. Stat. § 3516.	Silver dollar........	....	Interdicted.	-	-
§ 3513.	Silver dollar, fractions of.............	‡347.22	Five dollars.	-	-
§ 3513.	Silver "trade dollar".....................	378.00	§Five dollars.	16.27907 to 1......	About 15.9 to 1
§ 3511.	Gold dollar *and* multiples of......	23.22	Unlimited.		

* Eagles, half-eagles, and quarter-eagles.

† Half-dollars, quarters, dimes, and half-dimes.

‡ The act (February 12, 1873) prescribes the weight of the debased fractional silver coins in "grams," which another act (Revised Statutes, section 3570) defines to be 15.432 grains each.

§ The making of the trade-dollar a limited legal tender by section 3586 of the Revised Statutes is believed to have been unintentional.

THE VOICE OF AUTHORITY.

The voice of authority has ever been in favor of the double standard and opposed to the single. I have only time to quote some of the most eminent statesmen, economists, bankers, writers, and practical men on this subject:

ALEX. HAMILTON.—

"To annul the use of either of the metals as money is *to abridge the quantity of circulating medium*, and is liable to all the objections which arise from a comparison of the *benefits of a full, with the evils of a scanty, circulation*." (Report to Congress, 1791.)

THOS. JEFFERSON.—

"I return you the report on the mint. I concur with you that the unit *must stand on both metals*." (Letter to Hamilton, February, 1792.)

LEON FAUCHET.—In his "*Recherches sur l'or et sur l'argent*," 1843, Leon Fauchet said:

"If all the nations of Europe adopted the system of Great Britain, the price of gold would be raised beyond measure, and we should see produced in Europe a result lamentable enough. The Government cannot decree that legal tender shall be only gold, in place of silver, for that would be to decree a revolution, and the most dangerous of all, because it would be a revolution leading to unknown results (*qui marcherait vers l'inconnu.*)"

M. WOLOWSKI.—In a memoir read before the French Institute in 1868 M. Wolowski said:

"The suppression of silver would bring on a veritable revolution. Gold would augment in value with a rapid and constant progress, which would break the faith of contracts, and aggravate the situation of all debtors, including the nation. It would add at one stroke of the pen at least three milliards to the twelve milliards of the public debt."

Though the voices and votes of this great statesman and publicist, and of those who sided with him in the debates of the Monetary Convention of 1865, were overpowered, yet they still reverberate throughout the world, for truth and right cannot be suppressed.

BARON DE ROTHSCHILD.—A monetary commission appointed by the French Government in 1869 took the testimony of practical financiers, who were unanimous against the proposed demonetization of silver. Before this commission M. le Baron Alphonse de Rothschild said:

"The actual state of things, that is to say, the simultaneous employment of the two precious metals, is satisfactory and gives rise to no complaint. What is most needed in commerce is facility in its operations, and to-day it employs, according to its needs, sometimes gold and sometimes silver, and the partial replacement of silver by gold, which has taken place in these later times, has been effected without inconvenience."

"They now demand that silver should be demonetized, as fifteen years ago they demanded that gold should be. The French government wisely refused to demonetize gold then, and it will be equally wise to refuse to demonetize silver now. In fact, whether gold or silver dominates for the time being, it is always true that the two metals concur together in forming the monetary circulation of the world, *and it is the general mass of the two metals combined which serves as the measure of the value of things.* In countries with the double standard the principal circulation will always be established of that metal which is the most abundant. It is scarcely twenty years ago that silver was the principal element in our transactions. Since the discoveries of the California and Australian mines, it is gold which has taken its place. No person can forsee what the future has in store for us, or can predict that the proportion in which the two metals are now produced may not be changed in favor of silver."

"It appears to me that there are real advantages in maintaining silver in circulation and none in its suppression, since it is now actually a part of the circulation. I should regret the demonetization of silver in its relations to our internal circulation, our commercial intercourse with other countries, and the always uncertain eventualities of the future. *But I should regret it even more if our example should be followed by other nations, for that suppression of silver would amount to a veritable destruction of values without any compensation.*"

"Without doubt the two metals are not always in the same measure at our control; there is always one more abundant than the other; but neither of them has ever completely disappeared, and we have always been able to find the one of which we had need."

This is not the voice of plutocracy; it is the utterance of a great financial Power, whose self-interest is grand, enlightened, and in harmony with the other great interests of the world.

M. D'EICHTAL.—M. d'Eichtal, a director of the Bank of France, said:

"In cotton, every fall in price brings an increase in consumption. But in silver, if you take away its title of legal money, which makes an unlimited outlet for it, it must fall exceedingly low before it would find an employment equal to the one you take away."

M. ROULAND.—M. Rouland, the Governor of the Bank of France, said:

"We have not to do with ideal theories. The two moneys have actually coexisted since the origin of human society, without any disadvantage, and even with actual advantage in all countries which have availed themselves of them. They coexist *because the two together are necessary, by their quantity, to meet the needs of circulation. This necessity of the two metals, has it ceased to exist?* Is it established that the quantity of actual and prospective gold is such that we can now renounce the use of silver without disaster? In place of the two moneys, is it entirely sure that the whole world can be usefully served with only one?"

M. WOLOWSKI.—M. Wolowski said:

"To adopt one metal, gold, to the exclusion of the other, it is not merely as if they closed all existing mines of silver, but as if they suppressed in this regard the labor of all past ages. The sum total of the precious metals is reckoned at fifty milliards,* one-half gold and one-half silver. If, by a stroke of the pen, they suppress one of these metals in the monetary service, they double the demand for the other metal, *to the ruin of all debtors.*"

M. DUMAS.—At the sitting of the French Senate on the 28th of January, 1870, which has properly been characterized as "memorable," from the magnitude of the subject of the debate, and from the

---

* M. Wolowski here refers not to coin only, but to the precious metals in coin *and* plate, &c.

dignity and gravity with which the discussion was maintained. Dumas, a Senator, to whose words learning, experience, virtue, and age combined to give weight, invoked the body to pause before concluding to make a change which "*would affect the whole human race.*" He said:

"Those who approach these questions for the first time decide them at once. Those who study them with care hesitate. Those who are obliged practically to decide, doubt and stop, overwhelmed with the weight of the enormous responsibility.

"The quantities of the precious metals which are now sufficient may become insufficient, and we should proceed with great prudence before we diminish that which constitutes a part of the riches of the human race. Sometimes gold takes the place of silver. Sometimes silver takes the place of gold. *This keeps up the general equilibrium.* Nobody can guarantee that the present vast production of gold will continue. The *placers* are found on the surface of the earth, and may be exhausted by the very facility of working them. Silver presents itself in the form of subterranean veins. Science may contribute to accelerate its extraction. In presence of the unknown, which dominates the future, we should practice a prudent reserve."

HENRI CERNUSCHI, the eminent French political economist and author of *La Monnaie Bimetallique*, writes an article in the Paris *Siecle* on the depreciation of silver, urging England and America to adopt a double standard, and to fix the relative value of gold and silver at 15½ to 1—the rate generally prevalent on the Continent. Dwelling specially on Anglo-Indian interests, M. Cernuschi says:

"Seduced by gold 'monometalism,' Europe has ceased to coin silver, but it had long coined it previously, and colossal sums are in circulation. All this silver is to be called in and melted down, the more so as it circulates as a forced currency for a value it no longer possesses. All this silver is to be sold, and it is to London it will be sent to get gold. Floods of silver going up the Thames, floods of gold descending; scarcity and increasing value of the yellow metal, which is the only English currency, glut and depreciation of the white metal, which is the only Indian currency—the two conflicting 'monometalisms' are about to face each other—the one suffering from anæmia, the other from plethora; two crises instead of one—a gold crisis and a silver crisis. From Galle to the Indus what a monetary shock, what a rise of prices produced by the invasion of silver! What increasing alterations in the value of all contracts and all engagements fixed in rupees! The most terrible monetary storm ever known, breaking out in a conquered country, amid a population six times as large as that of the United Kingdom! Can England fold her arms? Can she say to trembling interests, 'Be patient; everything will end by finding its level?' The indifferent fatalism to which somnolent ulemas may resign themselves is repugnant to the proud British Neptune. England will have resolution to eliminate the evil. To insure her welfare, she will desire all that is possible, rational, and efficacious. If it is demonstrated that the international rehabilitation of silver is the real solution, England will not hesitate; she will convoke the nations to the congress of monetary peace."

R. H. **PATTERSON**, a distinguished political economist, says:

"It appears evident, then, that the formidable objections which theorists make to the existence of a double standard of value in a country are unsupported by facts. They conjure up a vision of 'hydras, gorgons, and chimeras dire for which we feel no apprehension. If a country has enough of gold or of silver to make its coinage entirely of that metal, good and well. But if not—as is the case in India—by all means let it employ both metals. The correctness of this opinion is abundantly shown in the case of France. In that most logical of countries the double standard has long been established, and no one there has any desire to abolish it. During the last dozen years this double standard has been subjected to the severest test that could be applied, and yet every one is satisfied with its working. Gold is pouring in; silver is pouring out; a revolution is being effected in the currency of France; yet no one complains. Evidently practical or appreciable disadvantage of any kind is quite unknown. Theoretically, as we have shown, a double standard cannot do much harm; practically, we find, it does none at all. And since it works under the most trying circumstances without the least injury in France, it may safely be introduced without any apprehension and with great advantage into India."—R. H. Patterson, *The Economy of Capital*, London, 1864, p. 59.

ERNEST SEYD. This able and impartial writer has written several works on coin and bullion which evince a thorough knowledge of these difficult subjects. He says:

"The rejection of silver as a standard of value would be a most unwise and dangerous proceeding. It would be a far better and safer course to establish the double gold and silver valuation."—*Bullion and Foreign Exchanges*, London, 1868.

"We think it can be shown that the gold valuation has been injurious to England's interests in her foreign trade as well as in her internal financial policy." Ibid.

Similar views are entertained in Mr. Seyd's latest essay published in the Journal of the Society of Arts for March, 1876.

CONCLUSION.

I have done. For the patience and attention with which Senators have listened to an exposition unusually lengthy and somewhat tedious, I thank them, and can only plead the transcendent importance of the subject.

There is yet time to undo the work of 1873, to correct the grave blunder perpetrated by the Mint Act of that year, in interdicting the American silver dollar and substituting the single standard of gold for the money of the Constitution. The disastrous effects which, in my opinion, are bound to flow from this attenuation of the standard and the basis of prices and credit, are not yet felt; because of the existing suspension of specie payments. But so soon as specie payments are resumed—if, indeed, they can ever be resumed without the restoration and co-ordination of silver in the standard—will the bad effects of this legislation develop themselves and make their mark upon the affairs of the country. It may then be too late to reform.

The present is therefore the acceptable time to undo the unwitting and inconsiderate work of 1873, and to render our legislation upon the subject of money consistent with the physical facts concerning the stock and supply of the precious metals throughout the world, and conformable to the Constitution of the country.

We cannot, we dare not, avoid speedy action upon this subject. Not only do reason, justice, and authority unite in urging us to retrace our steps; but the organic law commands us to do so; and the presence of peril enjoins what the law commands. By idly interfering with the standard of the country, Congress has led the nation away from the realms of prosperity and thrust it beyond the boundaries of safety. To refuse to replace it upon its former vantage-ground, would be, to incur a responsibility and deserve a reproach, greater than that which men have ever before felt themselves able to bear.

APPENDIX.

MOVEMENT OF THE CURRENCY.

Table A, showing the currency of the United States from 1775 to 1875, inclusive. Sums in millions of dollars and tenths.

YEAR.	COIN.	UNITED STATES AND NATIONAL BANK NOTES.	STATE BANK NOTES.	TOTAL PAPER.	TOTAL CURRENCY.	POPULATION.	CURRENCY, PER CAPITA.	REMARKS.
1775	$6.0	....	....	$5.0	$11.0	2.5	$4.40	Lord Sheffield (Seybert, 554) says 9½ coin.
1775–1781	....	....	....	....	....	....	....	Era of "Continental money."
1790	16.0	$2.0	$1.0	3.0	19.0	3.9	4.87	Repudiation of Continental issues.
1791	16.0	....	....	9.0	25.0	4.0	6.25	First bank U. S.
1792	17.0	5.0	2.0	7.0	24.0	4.1	5.85	
1793	20.0	....	....	11.0	31.0	4.3	7.20	
1794	21.5	....	....	11.5	33.0	4.5	7.40	
1795	19.0	....	....	11.0	30.0	4.6	6.50	
1796	16.5	....	....	10.5	27.0	4.8	5.60	
1797	16.0	....	....	10.0	26.0	4.9	5.30	Suspension Bank England; flux of gold.
1798	14.0	....	....	9.0	23.0	5.0	4.60	
1799	17.0	....	....	10.0	27.0	5.2	5.20	Expiration of charter of First Bank United States.
1800	17.5	....	....	10.5	28.0	5.3	5.30	
1801	17.0	....	....	11.0	28.0	5.5	5.10	
1802	16.5	....	....	10.0	26.5	5.7	4.70	
1803	16.0	....	....	11.0	27.0	5.9	4.60	
1804	17.5	....	....	14.0	31.5	6.1	5.30	
1805	18.0	....	....	15.0	33.0	6.3	5.20	
1806	18.5	....	....	17.0	35.5	6.5	5.50	
1807	20.0	....	....	18.0	38.0	6.7	5.70	Embargo Dec. 22; first steamboat.
1808	20.0	....	....	22.75	44.7	6.9	6.40	
1809	20.0	....	....	24.0	44.0	7.0	6.10	Specie drain; Mexican disturbances; stoppage of mines; suspension N. E. banks.
1810	19.0	....	....	26.0	45.0	7.1	6.10	Drain of specie.
1811	18.0	....	....	28.0	46.0	7.3	6.10	Apprehension of war. (Drain of specie.)
1812	17.0	....	....	35.0	52.0	7.6	6.80	War declar'd with England.
1813	17.0	....	....	52.0	69.0	7.8	8.80	War continued; bank mania.
1814	17.0	....	....	51.5	69.5	8.0	8.70	August and September all except N. E. b'ks suspended until January, 1817. Gold 114 @ 120.
1815	20.0	....	....	45.5	65.5	8.2	8.00	February, peace. Gold 115 @ 102.
1816	24.5	....	....	50.0	74.5	8.4	8.80	Gold 116 @ 117, 107; second bank U. S.; England adopts the gold standard.
1817	*22.0	....	....	55.0	77.0	8.6	8.90	Partial resumption of Bank United States.
1818	*20.0	....	....	60.0	80.0	8.8	9.00	Height of bank mania; gold drain.

*In these years the coin was all of silver; no gold. (Report of Mr. White, H. Rep., 21st Cong., 2d sess., No. 95.) In the year 1830 coins in bank $15,000,000, silver in circulation $8,000,000, bank notes $77,000,000; total $100,000,000. (Senate Rep., 21st Cong., 2d sess., Dec. 5, 1830, by Mr. Sanford, from Select Com. on Cur.)

Table A—Continued.

YEAR.	COIN.	UNITED STATES AND NATIONAL BANK NOTES.	STATE BANK NOTES.	TOTAL PAPER.	TOTAL CURRENCY.	POPULATION.	CURRENCY, PER CAPITA.	REMARKS.
1819	*20.0	....	....	62.5	82.5	9.1	9.20	Revulsion.
1820	*26.5	....	....	58.0	86.0	9.4	9.00	Resumption of Bank of England; continued efflux of gold from United States.
1821	*23.0	....	....	65.0	88.0	9.7	9.10	Spring strict're. (Tucker, p. 208, says 18. to 20. coin.)
1822	*18.0	....	....	70.0	88 0	10.0	8.80	
1823	*17 0	....	....	76.0	93.0	10.3	9.00	
1824	*18.0	....	....	78.0	96.0	10.6	9.10	
1825	*19.0	....	....	81.0	100.0	10.9	9.20	
1826	*20.0	....	....	80.0	100.0	11.1	9.00	Tempor'y bank panic.
1827	*22.5	....	....	75.0	97.5	11.5	8 50	Winter stricture.
1828	*27.0	....	....	68.0	95.0	11.9	8.00	First railway in U. S.
1829	*31.0	12.5	50.0	62.5	83.5	12.4	7.50	Temporary bank panics; Pres. Jackson declares against re-chartering United States Bank.
1830	*32.0	....	....	61.0	93.0	12.8	7.20	Report of Cong. Com. favoring bank.
1831	35.0	....	....	66.0	101.0	13.2	7.65	Bill introduced to re-charter bank.
1832	39.0	....	....	71.0	110.0	13.6	8.10	
1833	42.7	....	....	77.0	119.7	14.0	8.50	Removal of deposits from bank.
1834	60.0	....	....	90.0	150.0	14.4	10.40	Veto of bank bill.
1835	80.0	....	....	103.0	183.0	14.8	12.40	Great fire in New York; loss, $20,000,000.
1836	65.0	....	....	140.0	205.0	15.3	13.30	Expiration of charter of Second Bank U. S.
1837	73.0	....	....	149.0	222.0	15.8	14.00	GREAT SUSPENSION.
1838	87.0	....	....	116.0	203.0	16.2	12.50	Universal insolvency; banker's repudiation of Morris canal stock; general contraction; fall in prices; stay laws; bankr'p'y laws; liquidation; riots.
1839	87.0	....	....	135.0	222.0	16.7	13.40	
1840	83.0	....	....	107.0	190 0	17.0	11.20	
1841	80.0	....	....	107.0	187.0	17.5	10.70	
1842	60.0	....	....	83.7	143.7	18.0	8.00	Repudiation of the States.
1843	70.0	....	....	58.5	128.5	18.6	6.90	Lowest depression; resumption.
1844	100.0	....	....	75.0	175.0	19.2	9.10	Increase of currency.
1845	96.0	....	....	90.0	186.0	19.8	9.40	
1846	97.0	....	....	105.5	202.5	20.4	9.90	
1847	120.0	....	....	105.5	225.5	21.0	10 07	
1848	112 0	....	....	128.5	240.5	21.6	11.10	California mines opened.
1849	120.0	....	....	114.7	234.7	22.4	10.50	
1850	154.0	....	....	131.0	285.0	23.2	12.20	
1851	186.0	....	....	155.0	341.0	24.0	14.20	
1852	204.0	....	....	156.0	360.0	24.8	14.50	
1853	236.0	....	....	144.0	380.0	25.6	14.80	
1854	240.0	....	....	178.6	418.6	26.4	15.80	Australian mines.
1855	257.6	....	....	187.0	444.6	27.1	16.40	
1856	250.2	....	....	196.0	446.2	27.7	16.10	
1857	259.3	....	....	215.0	474.3	28.4	16.70	Temporary panic; suspension.
1858	251.6	....	....	155.0	406.6	29.1	14.00	Resumption.
1859	265.8	....	....	193.0	458.8	29.7	15.40	
1860	257.0	....	....	207.0	457.0	31.5	14.50	
1861	241.4	....	....	202.0	443.4	32.3	13.70	Civil war; demand notes issued.

* In these years the coin was all of silver; no gold. (Report of Mr. White, H. Rep., 21st Cong., 2d sess., No. 95.) In the year 1830 coins in bank $15,000,000, silver in circulation $8,000,000, bank notes $77,000,000; total $100,000,000. (Senate Rep., 21st Cong., 2d sess., Dec. 5, 1830, by Mr. Sanford, from Select Com. on Cur.)

Table A—Continued.

Year.	Coin.	United States and national bank notes.	State bank notes.	Total paper.	Total currency.	Population.	Currency, per capita.	Remarks.
1862	298.5	....	....	184.0	482.5	22.9	21.00	SUSPENSION; greenbacks issued.
1863	100.0	411.0	161.0	572.0	672.0	24.5	27.40	Circulation of State banks supplanted by national banks.
1864	90.0	513.0	140.0	653.0	743.0	26.1	28.50	National bank notes; highest inflation. Gold 285.
1865	85.0	604.0	65.0	669.0	754.0	30.3	24.90	Peace; gradual contraction.
1866	100.0	713.0	37.0	750.0	850.0	†36.0	23.60	Rehabilitation of the South.
1867	140.0	704.0	nom.	704.0	844.0	†37.0	22.80	Extinction of State bank circulation.
1868	140.0	699.0	nom.	699.0	839.0	†38.0	22.00	Contraction continues slowly.
1869	140.0	692.0	nom.	692 0	832.0	‡39.1	21.20	Contraction continues slowly.
1870	152.8	704.0	nom.	704.0	856.4	38.6	22.20	
1871	136.7	723.7	nom.	723.7	860.4	39.6	21.70	Great Chicago fire; loss $150,000,000.
1872	128.1	741.4	nom.	741.4	869.5	40.6	21.40	Great Boston fire; loss $80,000,000.
Jan. '73	130.0	752.0	nom.	752.0	882.0	41.7	21.10	Silver demonetized;
Oct. '73	140.0	762.0	20.0	872.0	922.0	41.7	22.10	panic; $20,000,000 clearing-house certificates and $10,000 000 Treasury reserves issued as currency; gold imp'rt'd.
1874	140.0	761.1	nom.	761.1	901.1	42.9	21.00	Contraction contin'ed.
1875	142.0	736.3	nom.	736.3	878.3	44.1	19.90	Contraction contin'ed

†According to censuses taken in 1866, 1867, and 1868 by the Bureau of Statistics through the Internal Revenue organization. The census of 1870 shows a smaller population than that of 1869, but the discrepancy is attributed to the different means and methods adopted to effect the enumeration. The figures subsequent to 1870 are based upon the census of that year.

‡Estimate based on census of 1868.

FAILURES IN BUSINESS.

The following table (B) is from the Mercantile Agency Reports, and shows that the number of failures in business in all the States of the Union has closely followed the movement of the currency:

Year.	Movement of Currency.	Failures.
1859	Increasing	3,913
1860	Increasing	3,673
1861	Decreasing	6,993
1862	Increasing	1,652
1863	Increasing	485
1868	Decreasing	2,608
1869	Decreasing	2,799

Table B—Continued.

Year.	Movement of Currency.	Failures.
1870	Decreasing	3,551
1871	Decreasing	2,915
1872	Decreasing	4,060
1873	Decreasing	5,183
1874	Decreasing	5,830
1875	Decreasing	7,740

There were but few failures during the rapid increment of the currency from 1862 to 1866. Since that period the number of failures has steadily and largely increased, until now it is 7,740 per annum, and during the first three months of 1876 it was 2,806, or at the rate of 11,224 per annum.

The failures in New York City, taken by itself, were as follows: 1871, 324; 1872, 385; 1873, 644; 1874, 645; 1875, 951; and during the first three months of 1876, 313.

TABLE C—FIRES IN NEW YORK CITY.

Period.	No. of years in period.	Currency during the period.	Av'g annual No. fires.
1856–'60	5	Increasing	653
1861	1	Decreasing	827
1862–'66	5	Increasing	720
1867	1	Decreasing	1,012
1868	1	Decreasing	912
1869	1	Decreasing	914
1870	1	Decreasing	867
1871	1	Decreasing	916
1872	1	Decreasing	922
1873	1	Decreasing	1,017
1874	1	Decreasing	841
1875	1	Decreasing	1,093

Annual average, 1867 to 1875, inclusive, 944

The number of these fires which were of incendiary origin are only given for the years 1855 to 1860, inclusive. They were as follows: 1855, 159; 1856, 100; 1857, 87; 1858, 90; 1859, 68; 1860, 110. The ratio of incendiary to total fires during this period was about 30 per cent. According to the New York Insurance Reports it is believed to be now over 50 per cent.

MARRIAGES.

The correspondence between marriages and the price of bread-corn was shown statistically some forty years ago by the illustrious Quetelet. The following table shows the correspondence between marriages and the movement of the currency. Ohio is one of the few States of the Union in which social statistics are compiled under official authority:

Table D, showing the number of Marriages in Ohio.

Year.	Movement of currency.	Marriages.
1859	Increasing	22,671
1860	Perturbation	23,106
1861	Decreasing	22,251
1862	Increasing	19,540
1863	Increasing	19,300
1864	Increasing	20,881
1865	Increasing	22,198
1866	Increasing	30,479
1867	Decreasing	29,230
1868	Decreasing	28,231
1869	Decreasing	23,910
1870	Decreasing	25,459
1871	Decreasing	24,627
1872	Decreasing	26,303
1873	Decreasing	26,460
1874	Decreasing	26,678
1875	Decreasing	27,047

The population of the State of Ohio was in 1850 1,980,-329, in 1860 2,339,511, and in 1870 2,665,260.

The decrease of marriages accompanying the diminution of currency which has gone on since 1866 is complemented by a corresponding increase of divorces.

DIVORCES.

Table E, showing the number of Divorces in Ohio.

Year.	Currency.	Divorces.
1866–1869 (average 3 years)	Decreasing	1,003
1870	Decreasing	1,008
1871	Decreasing	1,077
1872	Decreasing	1,026
1873	Decreasing	1,124
1874	Decreasing	1,159
1875	Decreasing	1,299

The above evidences of "hard times" are supplemented by the statistics of desperate and criminal acts, all of which have constantly diminished whilst the currency of the country was increasing, and increased whilst the currency was decreasing.

HOMICIDES AND SUICIDES.

Table F, showing the number of inquests held upon Homicides and Suicides in Ohio.

Period.	Currency.	Homicides and suicides.
1858–1860 (average 3 years) ...	Increasing	144
1861	Decreasing	190
1862–1865 (average 4 years) ...	Increasing	162
1866–1869 (average 4 years) ...	Decreasing	182
1870	Decreasing	162
1871	Decreasing	128
1872	Decreasing	211
1873	Decreasing	206
1874	Decreasing	219
1875	Decreasing	261

SUICIDES.

Table G, showing the Suicides in the City of New York.

Year.	Currency.	Suicides.
1866	Decreasing	58
1867	Decreasing	76
1868	Decreasing	98
1869	Decreasing	102
1870	Decreasing	101
1871	Decreasing	114
1872	Decreasing	144
1873	Decreasing	118
1874	Decreasing	–
1875	Decreasing	157

Table H, showing the Suicides in the City of Philadelphia.

Year.	Suicides.	Average.	Currency.
1860	–	20	Perturbation.
1861	–	31	Decreasing.
1862	14	22	Increasing.
1863	24		Increasing.
1864	20		Increasing.
1865	31		Increasing.
1866	44	38	Decreasing.
1867	35		Decreasing.
1868	29		Decreasing.
1869	45		Decreasing.
1870	25		Decreasing.
1871	41		Decreasing.
1872	48		Decreasing.
1873	–	47	Decreasing.
1874	–	59	Decreasing.
1875	–	68	Decreasing.

PRISONERS.

Table I, showing the number of persons in prison in all the United States in June of each of the years 1850, 1860, *and* 1870, *such being the periods at which the last three decennial censuses were taken.*

Period.	Movement of currency.	Population.	Persons in prison.
1850	Increasing	23,191,876	6,737
1860	Perturbation	31,443,323	19,086
1870	Decreasing	38,558,371	32,904

INDEX.

www.ingramcontent.com/pod-product-compliance
Lightning Source LLC
LaVergne TN
LVHW011238110826
845150LV00006B/1674